Hello and welcome!

Dein *Wordmaster*-Heft hilft dir beim Wörterlernen.

In der Schule lernst du Englisch mit dem Buch *Go Ahead 6*.
Dort besprecht ihr auch die neuen Wörter einer Seite.

Danach machst du zuerst die Übung **New words** in deinem *Wordmaster*-Heft, die zu der neuen Seite in deinem Englischbuch gehört. Bei dieser Aufgabe fügst du die neuen Wörter in eine kleine Geschichte oder eine Unterhaltung ein und übst sie dadurch.

Wenn du mal nicht weiter weißt, darfst du im *Unit vocabulary* (Wörterverzeichnis) von *Go Ahead 6* (S.131–151) nachschauen.

Anschließend kannst du überprüfen, ob du alles richtig gelöst hast: Die Lösungen findest du im beigelegten Lösungsteil.

Wenn du sicher bist, dass die Lösung richtig ist, präge dir die Sätze ein. So behältst du die neuen Wörter besser!

Nach **New words** bietet der *Wordmaster* dann noch viele weitere Übungen zum Lernen der neuen Wörter, zum Beispiel Wortspiele und Rätsel.

Der *Wordmaster* gibt dir auch wichtige **Lerntipps** (auf Deutsch), die die Frage beantworten, wie man englische Wörter am besten lernt.

Am Ende jeder *Wordmaster*-Unit findest du dein **Learner log**, dein Lerntagebuch. Dort kannst du Fragen zu deinen Erfahrungen mit dem Wörterlernen beantworten.

Viel Spaß beim Englischlernen!

1 New words ▸ p. 4

Find the English words for the German words in brackets and fill in the gaps.

Hi Donna, I'm in Munich at the moment. **1** Like London, Munich is a very __________ *(lebendige)* _______ *(Großstadt)*. **2** There are many _____________ *(berühmte)* ____________ *(Sehenswürdigkeiten)* in the ____________________ *(Stadtzentrum)*. **3** On Marienplatz, you can listen to 43 _________ *(Glocken)*! **4** There's also a very large ____________ *(Palast)* near the ____________ *(Zentrum)*. It's called the Residenz. **5** You can see other ______________________ *(interessante)* things when you take a bus________ *(Busrundfahrt)*. **6** It takes you to the Olympic[1] __________ *(Turm)*. (Yes, Munich had Olympic Games, too!) **7** Munich has also got an old ____________ *(Gefängnis)*, like London. **8** But it's not very _______________ *(spannend, aufregend)*. **9** Like in London, you can walk ____ *(an)* a _________ *(Fluss)*, the _________ *(Fluss)* Isar. **10** You can see many old and new ______________ *(Brücken)* and the _____________ *(berühmte)* Bavarian[2] _____________________ *(Parlament)*. Munich has got many parks, too. **11** They're very ___________ *(lebendige)* places. **12** Sometimes you can see ______________________ *(Feuerschlucker/innen)* and _______________ *(Jongleur/innen)* there. I really like Munich! When you come to Germany again, we can go there together.

Love, Korbinian

2 Tips for London

Look at the four adjectives in the box. Then read each tip carefully and complete it with the ***best*** *adjective.*

exciting • famous • interesting • lively

1 When you're in London, go to Covent Garden. There's a really good fire-eater there. His name is Fernando. Many people know him. He's ______________________!

2 When you're in London, take a bus tour of the sights. Why? Because you can sit down, see the sights – and listen. The information on the buses is always very ______________________.

3 When you're in London, you must go to the Tower of London. It's a very old prison. You can visit it. It's so ______________________!

4 Do you come from a small, quiet town? London is the opposite! It's full of life and activity. Like other big cities, London is very ______________________.

[1] **Olympic** [ə'lɪmpɪk] olympisch   [2] **Bavarian** [bə'veərɪən] bayerisch

3 Word ladder

Go up the ladder step by step. Change (only) one letter each time.
(Klettere Stufe für Stufe die Leiter hinauf. Ändere jedes Mal (nur) einen Buchstaben.)

7 Who's there? Mum? I can't hear you. Let's ★ later.

6 It isn't far to the Tower of London. You can ★ there.

5 I've got some photos of London on the ★ in my room.

4 Where's my London umbrella? – It's in the ★ .

3 Where in London can we play ★ ?

2 Big Ben isn't a tower, it's a ★ .

1 Excuse me, can you ★ me the way to Covent Garden?

4 Make the words

Take one piece from each of the two buses and complete the words.
***Tip:** All twelve words are from page 4 of your book.*

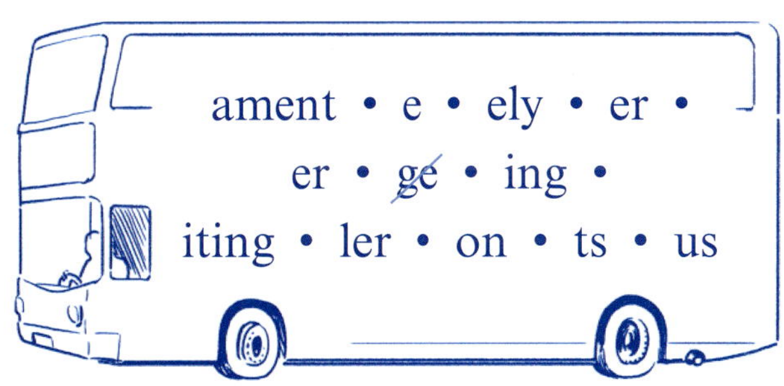

1	*bri*dge	4	*interes*	7	*pala*	10	*ri*
2	*ex*	5	*jug*	8	*parl*	11	*sig*
3	*fam*	6	*li*	9	*pri*	12	*to*

5 Jumbled sentences

Put the words in the right order.

1 of sights please? show ~~Can~~ London, you the me

Can ____________________

2 take I'd prison tour old to the a London. in like of

____

3 Hyde Park a on take Sunday. the Let's lake on in boat

____

6 New words ▸ p. 5

Find the English words for the German words in brackets and fill in the gaps.

At the tourist information[1]

Question **1** Which ______________________________ *(U-Bahn-Linie)*

goes from Westminster to Baker ___________ *(Straße)*, please?

Answer **2** That's the __________________ *("Kreislinie")*.

Question **3** Is the __________ *(Königin)* at Buckingham Palace at the moment?

Answer No, she isn't. Sorry!

Question What's the O_2?

Answer It's a large place for sports and music events[2]. **4** It was called the ____________________ ________ *(Jahrtausendkuppel)* from 1999–2005. It's very exciting.

Question **5** How do I get from ____________ *(Zentral-)* London to Greenwich?

Answer **6** Greenwich is in the ____________________ *(Südosten)*.

7 You can take the ______ *(U-Bahn)*.

Question **8** Can you really _________ *(bauen)* a bridge with _______ *(Holz)* and _______ *(Lehm)*?

Answer Of course not! **9** __________ *(Ziegelsteine)* and ___________ *(Steine)* are also dangerous because there are too many cars.

7 Puzzle 'In London'

Look at the pictures and write the ten words. What's the mystery word?

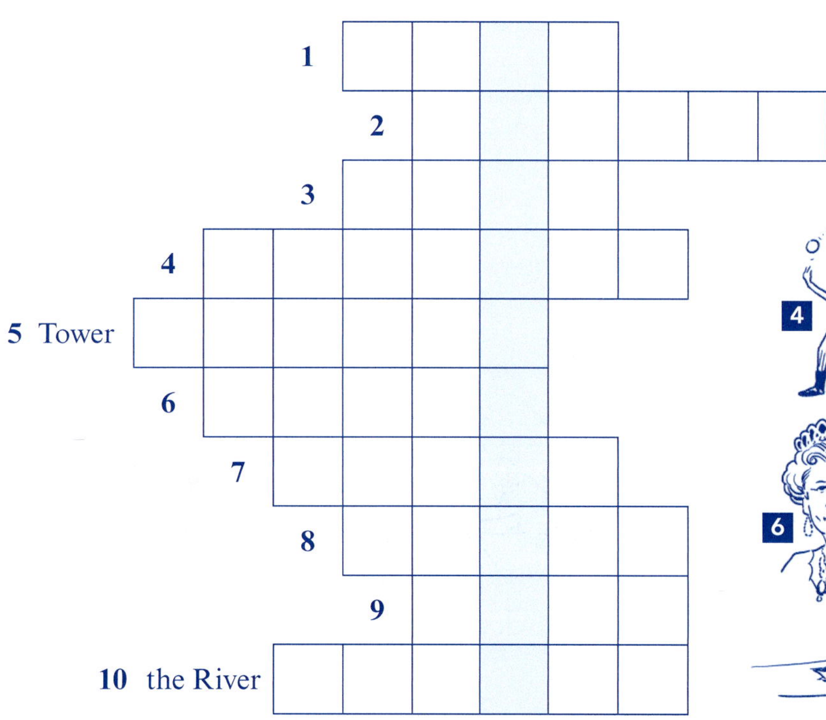

[1] **tourist** ['tʊərɪst] **information** Fremdenverkehrsamt [2] **event** [ɪ'vent] Veranstaltung, Ereignis

8 More questions and answers

Complete the questions with the right question word from the box. Then draw a line to the right answer.

how • what • when • where • which • who • whose • why

1 ____________ tube line goes from Paddington to Victoria?

2 ____________ far is it from here to the River Thames?

3 ____________ is the name of the bell in the tower?

4 ____________ can you see in Covent Garden?

5 ____________ is Greenwich?

6 ____________ does the next bus tour start?

7 ____________ home is Buckingham Palace?

8 ____________ is London so lively and exciting?

a) In south-east London.

b) Because it's a very big city.

c) The Circle Line.

d) About two miles.

e) In five minutes.

f) Big Ben.

g) Fire-eaters and jugglers.

h) The Queen's.

9 Word partners

Find the partner word. The words in the box below can help you.

1 quiet >< ______________________

2 boring >< ______________________

3 shed >< ______________________

4 tube >> ______________________

5 road >> ______________________

6 near >> ______________________

7 wood and ______________________

8 bricks and ______________________

9 south and ______________________

10 tower and ______________________

11 river and ______________________

12 circle and ______________________

bellbridgebyclayeastexcitinglivelylinepalacestonesstreetunderground

10 Odd word out

Which word does not fit? Cross it out.

1 brick – wood – ~~bell~~ – clay – stone

2 car – tour – underground – bus – tube

3 palace – tower – prison – circle – parliament

4 lady – queen – fire-eater – juggler – river

5 interesting – exciting – centre – famous – lively

11 New words ▸ p. 6

Find the English words for the German words in brackets and fill in the gaps. Put the names in the picture. Then find the answer to number 6.

1 Alex is Betty's ______________ *(Ehemann)*.

2 Alex and Betty have got a ______ *(Sohn)*, Connor.

3 Connor is Daisy's ____________ *(Cousin)*.

4 Daisy is Ellen's ________________ *(Tochter)*.

5 Ellen is Frank's ________ *(Ehefrau)*. Frank is Alex' brother.

6 So Ellen is Connor's . . . .

12 Families

This is a list of words for men and boys in a family. Put in the words for women and girls.

1 grandad	grandma	5 uncle	
2 husband		6 son	
3 father		7 brother	
4 dad		8 cousin	

13 Where are they?

You're at the tourist information in central London. Look at the map and complete the sentences.

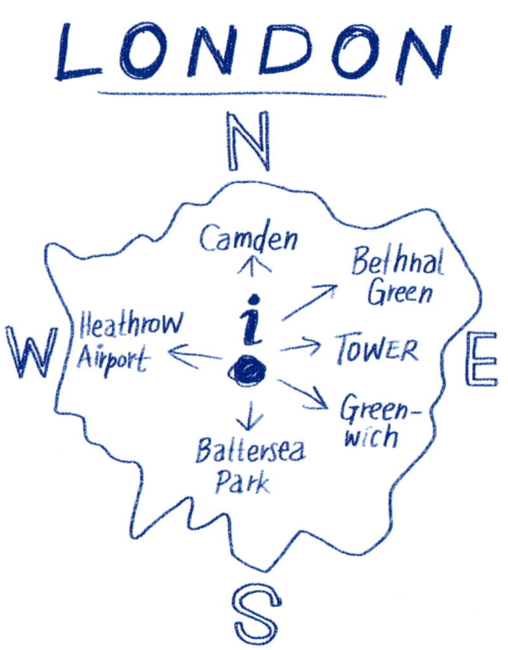

1 Greenwich is in ____________________ London.

You can go by boat or take the tube.

2 Battersea Park is interesting, too. It's __________ of here.

3 Camden is a good place to visit for young people.

It's __________ of here, not far.

4 It's a very interesting museum, not only for children.

It has got many old things. It's ____________________

of here, at Bethnal Green tube station.

5 Tower Bridge and the Tower are _______ of here. Let me show you on the map.

6 Heathrow Airport is in the ________. The tube goes there, but it takes about one hour.

14 New words ▸ p. 7

Find the English words for the German words in brackets and fill in the gaps.

1 There's a great ______________ *(Museum)* in London. **2** Not many ________________ *(Touristen)* know about it, but it's very ________________________ *(beliebt bei)* children. **3** It's called the '______________ *(Museum)* of Childhood[1]'. **4** It hasn't got _________________ *(Wachsfiguren)*, but it has got ____________ *(eine Menge, viele)* games, teddy bears and other things that children find interesting. **5** ___ *(Wenn, Falls)* there's a ___________ *(Warteschlange)*, it's usually __________ *(kurz)*. **6** And it's not just ___________ *(billig)* – it's free! **7** The best ______ *(Art und Weise)* to get there? Easy: Take the tube to Bethnal Green.

15 Definitions

What is it? Complete the definitions. Then find the mystery word.

1 Something is _ _ _ _ _ if you don't have to pay a lot for it.

2 Something is _ _ _ _ _ _ _ if a lot of people like it.

3 A film is _ _ _ _ _ if it's only five minutes long.

4 A person is a _ _ _ _ _ _ _ if he or she travels or visits a place in his/her free time.

5 A person is a _ _ _ _ _ _ _ _ _ _ if he or she plays football.

6 A place is a _ _ _ _ _ _ if you can go there and see a lot of pictures, old things or waxworks.

➜ London is ☐☐☐☐☐☐ for its lively city centre.
5 1 6 3 2 4

16 Sentences

Use a word from each box and make sentences. Use all the words, some of them two or three times.

eat | go | hear | see | visit   best | cheapest | famous | quickest   bell | food | people | sights | Tower | way

1 If you want to *see* the *best* *sights*, you must start in the city centre.

2 If you want to _______ the ___________ *way*, you must take the tube.

3 If you want to _______ ___________ ___________, you must go to Madame Tussaud's.

4 If you want to _______ the *famous* ___________, you must find the Houses of Parliament.

5 If you want to *visit* the ___________ ___________, you must pay a lot of money.

6 If you want to _______ the ___________ ___________, you must go to 'Ed's Cheaperia'.

[1] **childhood** ['tʃaɪldhʊd] Kindheit

17 New words ▸ p. 8

Find the English words for the German words in brackets and fill in the gaps.

Hi Uncle Jim. **1** On way to see you in London after ________________ *(Streit)* with Mum&Dad. **2** They're ________________ *(hoffnungslos)*!

3 ________________ *(Mach dir keine Sorgen)*.

4 Looking ________________ to *(Freue mich auf)* the big city. Love, Bill

Hi again. **5** Problem: train __________ *(Fahrkarte)* not in my __________ *(Tasche)*.

6 But ________________ *(mach dir keine Sorgen)*. **7** Train very ________ *(belebt)*.

All OK. In London now. **8** ________________ *(Mach dir keine Sorgen)*. **9** Going to ________________ *(Gruselkabinett)*. **10** You are best uncle in the __________ *(Welt)*!

Uncle Jim? **11** ________________ *(Mach dir keine Sorgen)*. **12** I can ________________ *(sich kümmern um)* myself[1]. **13** I'm ____ *(kein)* little kid. Where are you???

OK. On way home. **14** ________________ *(Mach dir keine Sorgen)*. See you in the summer.

18 Pronunciation

a) *Match the words in the box to the correct phonetic symbol.*

~~after~~ • cheap • cheese • circle • dance • daughter • door • eat • form • half • learn • part • shirt • street • walk • work

[ɑː]	[ɜː]	[ɔː]	[iː]
after			

b) *Match the words on the right to the phonetic symbols and find the mystery (silly) sentence.*

____

ðə ʃɔːt kwiːn əv ðɪ iːst ɪz

____

ðə best ɑːnt ɪn ðə wɜːld

[1] **myself** [maɪˈself] mich selbst

19 New words ▸ pp. 9–11

Find the English words for the German words in brackets and fill in the gaps.

1 If you go to England, you must always be very ____________ *(höflich)*. **2** English people use 'please' and 'thank you' _________ *(mehr)* ________ *(als)* other people. **3** And if you want to __________ *(überqueren)* the road, don't forget this ________ *(Regel)*: Always look right, then left, then right again! **4** Now put the _______________ *(fehlende)* word in this sentence: Cars drive on the ...... in England.

20 Word web

Write the English words for the German words below in the web. They all begin with p-.

1 arm
2 bitte
3 Flugzeug
4 Fußweg, Pfad
5 Gefängnis
6 höflich
7 öffentlich
8 Palast
9 schieben
10 Tasche
11 telefonieren
12 Teller

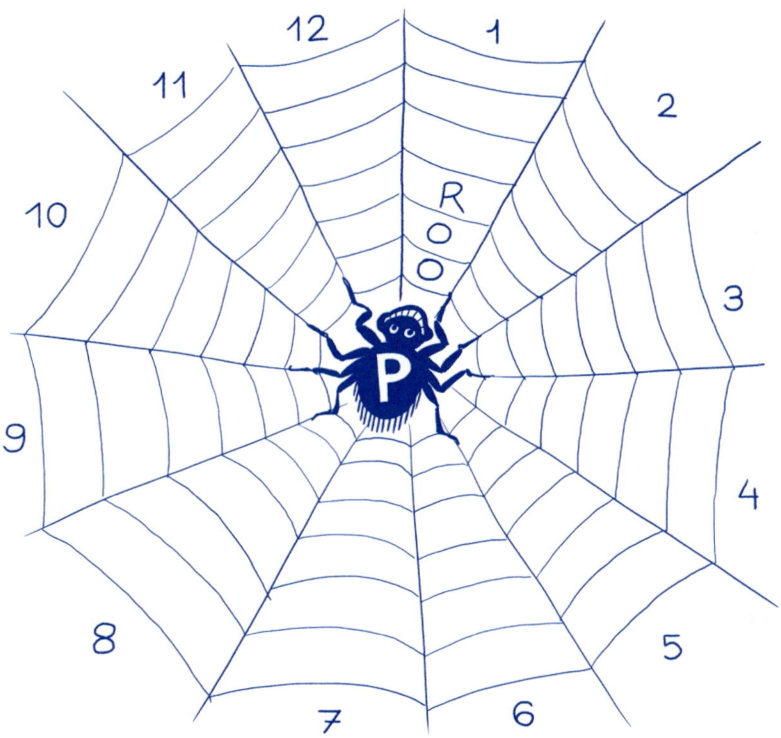

21 Definitions

Where in England can you see these rules? Match each rule with a place from the box below.

1 Always wear (all parts of) your uniform. No jeans, no T-shirts! B

2 If you have to wait, stand in a queue, please. _____

3 Don't throw your ticket away before the end of your journey. _____

4 Sh! Quiet, please. No shouting. No arguments. _____

5 Parents must look after their children. _____

6 Be careful: Look **right** – **left** – **right** before you cross the road in England. _____

A At a bus-stop • **B** At a school • **C** In a library • **D** In a tourist information
E In a train • **F** In the swimming-pool

22 New words ▸ pp. 12–13

Find the English words for the German words in brackets and fill in the gaps.

Ella **1** Can we play ______________ *(draußen)*?

Liam No, we can't. "It's raining cats and dogs again."

Ella What? **2** Where's the _______ *(Regen)* then? **3** Is this one of your silly __________ *(Witze)*?

Liam **4** My __________ *(Witze)* are ____________ *(besser)* than that. **5** It's the ____________ *(Slogan)* from the new ____________________________ *(Reklame)* for the Haddock Shopping Centre.

Ella Really? **6** It's ___ *(so …)* bad ___ *(… wie)* the shops there.

Liam **7** I think it's __________ *(schlechter)*! **8** It sounds old and ____________ *(langweilig)*.

Ella Yes. **9** And do you know the __________ *(schlechteste)* thing?

Liam What's that?

Ella It really is raining now – look!

23 Missing words

Complete the sentences.
Tip: *The words that you need are in the puzzle.*

B	A	S	Y	M	U	C	H	E	T	H	A	N	C	O
A	W	O	R	S	T	Y	R	M	O	R	E	N	L	D
C	H	V	E	R	Y	P	A	G	R	E	A	T	S	T
O	L	B	E	S	T	E	R	W	O	R	S	E	L	G

Hi, Mum and Dad! London is __________ (1).

It's _________ (2) better _________ (3) Passau! All the people here are ________ (4) friendly.

The museums aren't ___ (5) boring ___ (6) the museums in Passau. And the shops must be the ________ (7) shops in the world! OK, the weather is ___________ (8) ________ (9) at home. There's a lot of rain. And many things are _________ (10) expensive ________ (11) in Passau. The ___________ (12) prices[1] are for food. But I want to come back here ___ (13) often ___ (14) I can! Love, Sophie

Lerntipp

Am besten gehst du an Aufgaben immer so heran:
- Bleib ruhig – auch wenn du nicht sofort verstehst, worum es geht.
- Lies die Überschrift. Sie verrät dir oft schon, um was für eine Art von Übung es sich handelt.
- Lies die Arbeitsanweisung. Verstehst du sie? Lies sie noch einmal.
- Schau dir die Übung an. Manchmal siehst du sofort, was erwartet wird. Manchmal gibt es ein Beispiel.
- Trage die Lösungen erst einmal mit Bleistift ein, dann kannst du sie noch korrigieren.
- Nimm die Hilfen in Anspruch, die viele Übungen dir anbieten.
- Bei *Wordmaster*-Aufgaben: Schau dir die „New Words"-Übung an, die es oft oben auf der Seite gibt. Viele der gesuchten Wörter kommen dort vor.

[1] **price** ['praɪs] Preis

24 New words ▸ p. 14

Find the English words for the German words in brackets and fill in the gaps.

Ivan **1** What are all the people doing ____________________ *(dort drüben)*? **2** They ________ *(sehen … aus)* happy. **3** A lot of them are __________ ing *(lächeln)*. The TV is there, too. **4** Can you see the famous ____________________ *(Moderatorin)*?

Alma Yes, it's Maria Lopez. **5** Maybe they're waiting for the American ____________________ *(Präsidenten)*.

Ivan **6** No, I think they're fans of the __________ *(königliche)* family. **7** They're waiting for the ________ *(König)* and queen and their daughter, the _________________ *(Prinzessin)*.

Alma Oh, look. **8** Can you see Paolo, the ____________ *(Sänger)* ____________________ *(dort drüben)*? **9** ____________________ *(Er hat die Nase voll)*, I think. **10** Maybe because he's on his _______ *(ganz allein)* and no fan wants to talk to him.

Ivan **11** Imagine all these people are really waiting for some ___________________ *(Kriminelle)*. **12** They really want to see some ________________ *(fürchterliche, schreckliche)* _____________ *(Szenen)* of _______________ *(Folter)* and …

Alma What??!! What are you talking about??

Ivan **13** Well, in the Tower of London … oh, ____________________ *(vergiss es)*.

25 People and things

a) *Only half of these words (23) are words for people. Underline them.*

arcade aunt basket brick chess child clay cousin criminal daughter dome fire-eater footballer grandad husband idea joke journey juggler kid king kitchen lady order parents plate pocket presenter president princess queen racket relative river ruler shed singer son stamp subject sweater tourist tower umbrella wardrobe wife

b) *Use at least three of the words from a) and write a sentence.*

____

26 New words ▸ p. 15

Find the English words for the German words in brackets and fill in the gaps.

Carter How do you spell 'Hollywood'?

Lilly H-O-L-L-Y-W-O-O-D.

Carter Thanks. **1** That's nine ____________ *(Buchstaben)*, right?

Lilly Right. Why do you want to know?

Carter **2** Because Hollywood is looking for ____________ *(Fotomodelle)*. I'm writing to them.

Lilly **3** You – a __________ *(Fotomodell)*??

Carter No, not me, stupid. **4** One of our ________ *(Schweinen)*. She looks great. **5** I can ________ *(zeigen)* her to you when you come to the farm[1] on Saturday.

27 The right word

Underline the word that belongs in the sentence. Cross out the other two words.

1 We can't play outside today. The *weather* / ~~*letter*~~ / ~~*sister*~~ is too horrible.

2 Our alphabet has got 26 *lists* / *lessons* / *letters*.

3 I'm going to the post office. I need some stamps for these *rulers* / *letters* / *numbers*.

4 Let me *show* / *shout* / *smell* you round the house.

5 Lunch is ready. We're having *swing* / *stew* / *show* today.

6 There's a great *show* / *shop* / *shoe* on TV on Saturday.

Lerntipp

Erinnerst du dich? Jeder Mensch lernt anders. Weißt du inzwischen, was bei dir am besten wirkt?

- **Lesen und schreiben:** z.B. Wörterlisten anfertigen oder Sätze und kleine Geschichten schreiben.
- **Zeichnen:** z.B. Wortbilder erfinden oder Bedeutungen aufmalen.
- **Ordnen und sortieren:** z.B. eine Wortkartei führen oder Word Networks anfertigen.
- **Hören und sprechen:** z.B. mit CDs lernen oder sich gegenseitig abhören.
- **Spielen:** z.B. Memoryspiele oder Quartette anfertigen oder Wettspiele machen.

Was dir am meisten liegt, solltest du so oft wie möglich machen. So lernst du am besten.

[1] **farm** [fɑːm] Bauernhof

28 Network

Make a word network for 'In London'. The questions below and the words in the box can help you.

waxworks, museums, the Tower, … • visit, walk, see … • bus, tube, underground … • centre, south-east, Covent Garden …

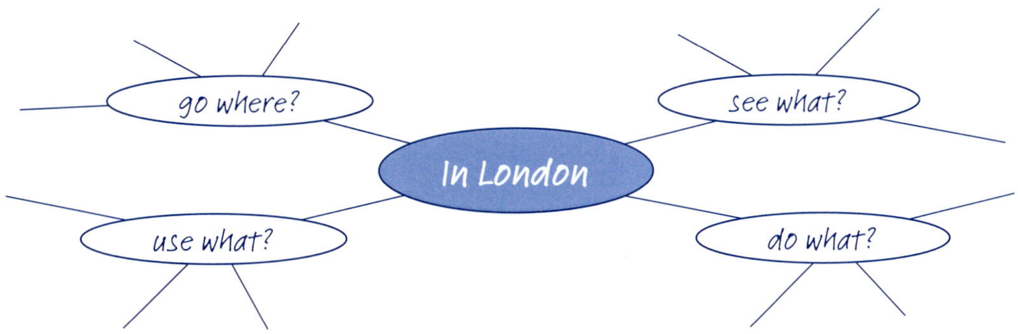

29 Word groups

Put the words in the grass below in the right bubble – in English, of course!

Tourists

They look at …

____

There are sights in the …

____

TV

You can see …

____

It's often …

____

aufregend Brücken Filme fürchterlich großartig interessant langweilig Moderatorinnen Museen Norden Osten Paläste Quizsendungen Reklamen Sänger Süden Türme Wachsfiguren Westen Zentrum

30 Crossword puzzle

Put the English words for the German words below in the crossword.

Across ▸
1 Teil
4 Brücke
5 beliebt
7 Regel
9 welche(r, s)
12 Warteschlange
15 Parlament
18 zeigen
20 kurz
21 Modell, Fotomodell
22 bauen

Down ▾
1 Schwein
2 Linie, Zeile
3 höflich
6 Streit
8 lebendig, rege, lebhaft
9 Weg
10 hoffnungslos
11 billig
13 fürchterlich, schrecklich
14 Kreis
16 beschäftigt, belebt
17 von, aus
19 Holz

31 The fourth[1] word

Find the fourth word and fill it in.
Tip: *The letters to the words are all in the box below – in the wrong order.*

1	horrible – awful	underground – tube	**5**	husband – wife	uncle – ________
2	better – worse	best – ________	**6**	north – south	east – ________
3	father – daughter	king – ________	**7**	waxwork – museum	criminal – ________
4	long – short	expensive – ________	**8**	president – king	parliament – ________

nuta • pahec • clappe • crispens • inpors • ~~ubte~~ • tews • strow

[1] **fourth** [fɔːθ] vierte/r/s

32 Three words

Complete each sentence with three words from the box. Careful! You don't need all the words.

a lot of • awful • ~~better~~ • boring • build • cheaper • cross • exciting • footballer • horrible • if • interesting • juggler • king • lively • missing • more • no • see • singer • which • worry • worse • worst

1 Look at that bike over there!

It's much better / ________________ / ________________ than my bike.

2 I never watch quiz shows on TV.

I think they're ________________ / ________________ / ________________!

3 Look, you can't ________________ / ________________ / ________________ the road here.

4 Don't you know Anna Soo?

She's a famous ________________ / ________________ / ________________.

5 Which is more ________________ / ________________ / ________________,

London's city centre or Munich's?

6 There are ________________ / ________________ / ________________ children in the park today.

MY LEARNER LOG

Mein Lerntagebuch. Hier notierst du deine Erfahrungen mit dem Wörterlernen.

♥ Meine drei englischen Lieblingswörter aus dieser Unit sind:

____

Diese drei Wörter kann ich mir von allen neuen Wörtern aus dieser Unit bisher am schlechtesten merken:

____

Dieses neue Wort / Diese neuen Wörter kannte ich schon:

____

Ich kann mir vorstellen, dass ich die neuen Wörter aus dieser Unit in folgenden Situationen gebrauchen kann:

– wenn ich selbst einmal nach London komme ☐

– wenn ich Touristen bei mir in der Stadt helfen will ☐

– wenn ich Städte oder Sehenswürdigkeiten miteinander vergleichen will ☐

und/oder: ____

1 New words ▸ p. 18

Find the English words for the German words in brackets and fill in the gaps.

Tom **1** My ______________________ *(Großeltern)* live in the ____________________

(auf dem Land). **2** They've got a ________ *(Bauernhof)*.

Selma Wow! **3** Have they got many pigs and ________ *(Kühe)*?

Tom No, they haven't.

Selma **4** Ah, they've got ____________ *(Pferde)* and ____________ *(Ponys)*, great!

Tom No, they haven't.

Selma No? **5** Well, have they got __________ *(Schafe)* and ________ *(Hennen, Hühner)*, then?

Tom **6** No, they haven't got ______________ *(Tiere)* on the _________ *(Bauernhof)*. They're too old for that, they say. They've got a dog and some cats, of course. **7** And they've got some ________________ *(Hütten, kleine Landhäuser)* for tourists and relatives. We often go there in the school holidays.

2 What is it?

Complete the sentences with the right animal word.

1 The ___________ is a big animal. It can often run fast. You can ride it.

2 The ___________ is a funny animal. It eats a lot. It's usually pink.

3 The ___________ is a big animal. It likes grass. We get most of our milk from it.

4 The ___________ is a pet when it lives in a flat. But on farms it usually lives outside. It likes mice.

5 The ___________ is smaller than its big "brothers and sisters" but it's not a small animal. Kids can ride it.

6 The ___________ is a useful animal. It likes grass. When you come near it, it usually runs away.

3 That can't be right!

Two (!) words are in the wrong place in each sentence. Cross them out and write the correct words.

1 The Newmans are farmers. They live on a big ~~country~~ farm in the ~~farm~~ country.

2 They've got some cottages for tourists and pigs. But they haven't got relatives or cows.

3 There are some rabbits behind their house. It's for their hutches.

4 Their budgies have got three daughters in a cage in their room.

4 New words ▸ p. 19

Find the English words for the German words in brackets and fill in the gaps.

We usually go to my grandparents' farm in the summer holidays. It's great. **1** If the weather is good, I walk to my favourite spot by a ____________ *(schönen, hübschen)* little ______________ *(Bach)* not far away from the farm. **2** When I _____ *(liege)* on the ______________ *(Boden)* and close my eyes, I can hear all the ___________ *(Vögel)* around me. **3** I can smell the _____ *(Luft)* and the _______________ *(Blumen)*, too. **4** When I open my eyes again, I can see the _________________ *(Schwalben)* in the sky. **5** Sometimes, when it's really quiet _______________________ *(überall)*, I can see a _________ *(Reh, Hirsch)*. **6** The ____________ *(jungen)* _________ *(Rehe, Hirsche)* are so ____________ *(schön, hübsch)*!

5 Funny animals

a) and b) don't belong together. Find the right b) for each a).

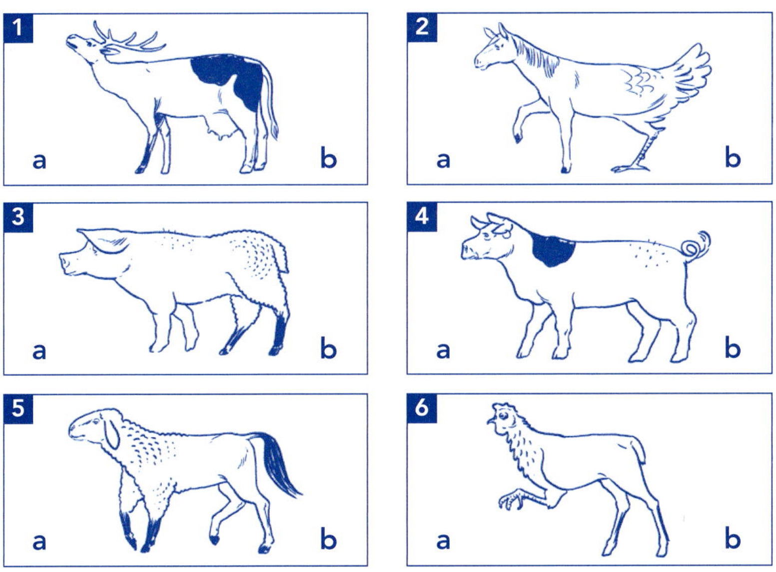

1a + 6b = deer
________ = ________
________ = ________
________ = ________
________ = ________
________ = ________

6 Right or wrong?

Are these sentences right (✔) or wrong (✘)?

1 Deer usually live on a farm. ☒
2 A stream is a very small river. ☐
3 You can often see birds in the sky. ☐
4 A pony is smaller than a horse. ☐
5 Grandparents are relatives. ☐
6 A swallow is a good pet. ☐
7 Pigs can fly. ☐
8 A cottage is a big country house. ☐
9 Cows and sheep often eat grass. ☐
10 A lot of flowers smell lovely. ☐

7 New words ▸ p. 20

Find the English words for the German words in brackets and fill in the gaps.

Hi Luke,

1 I wasn't at school ________________ *(gestern)* and today because I'm ____ *(krank)*.

2 _______ *(Letzte)* night I had a funny __________ *(Traum)*. I was outside and it rained. **3** So I ____________ *(wusch mir)* my _______ *(Haare)* in the rain! **4** _______________ *(Jede/r, Alle)* watched me. **5** _____________ *(Du warst)* there, too. **6** Then ______________ *(jemand)* shouted: '________ *(Hör auf)*!' **7** And I ______________ *(hörte auf)*. And that was it. Funny!

8 I want to write the __________ *(Traum)* in my _________ *(Tagebuch)*. I don't want to forget it. **9** Now I hope I can go to school again ________________ *(morgen)*. **10** We must finish our German _____________ *(Projekt)*.

See you, Dana

8 The right word

Complete the sentences with the right word from the "box".

are • aren't
is • isn't
~~were~~ • weren't
was • wasn't

Kevin Where were (1) you yesterday?

Alice I ____________ (2) at home.

Kevin At home? Why ____________ (3) you at school?

Alice Because my dog ____________ (4) ill. He can't eat his food.

Kevin What? Mr Brown ____________ (5) very happy yesterday, you know.

Alice Well, what can I do? My parents ____________ (6) usually at work all day.

And my grandparents ____________ (7) here at the moment.

Kevin Well, it ____________ (8) my problem. But Mr Brown can get very angry.

9 When?

Complete the sentences with **yesterday**, **today** *or* **tomorrow**.

1 The party ____________ was great. I danced with everyone. Then I had a funny dream about it later.

2 I'm going to bed now. I'd like to go to London early _______________, OK?

3 The weather is really wonderful _______________. Let's go outside.

4 I'm looking forward to _______________ when the summer holidays start – at last!

5 I watched a good film on TV _______________. It was really interesting.

10 New words ▸ p. 21

Find the English words for the German words in brackets and fill in the gaps.

Elena I'm so angry!

Karim Why? **1** What ________________ *(geschah)*?

Elena **2** In the ________ *(Vergangenheit)* we always went to the seaside in the summer holidays.

3 I lay on the beach and I enjoyed the ______ *(Meer)* and the ______ *(Sonne)*. It was wonderful!

Karim Sure. And what's the problem?

Elena This year my parents want to take us to the country. **4** They saw a silly little cottage in a silly little ____________ *(Dorf)* and they think it's great. **5** No beach, of course, only a stupid ____________ *(Wald)*!

Karim Don't worry. **6** We went to the country last summer and we ______ *(taten)* a lot of interesting things like geocaching[1]. It's fantastic!

11 Missing verbs

Complete the sentences with the right verb in the simple past form from the box.

did drove got saw rode said thought went

Last year we ____________ (1) to a little village in the country for the summer holidays. 'What a boring place,' I ____________ (2) when we ____________ (3) there. But then a lot of things happened.

I ____________ (4) a deer by the stream. I ____________ (5) a horse around the forest.

I ____________ (6) geocaching with other kids. And the best thing of all: I ____________ (7) a tractor! At the end of the holidays I ____________ (8) to my parents, "I'd really like to come back here next year."

Lerntipp

In der Liste „Irregular verbs" (*GO AHEAD 6*, S.152–153) kannst du die besonderen Vergangenheitsformen der unregelmäßigen Verben nachschlagen.

Steht ein Wort **nicht** in der linken Spalte, ist es **regelmäßig**. Solche Wörter brauchen für die einfache Vergangenheitsform *(simple past)* meist nur ihre Grundform und -ed, z.B. *work: I worked*.

Die besonderen Formen der **unregelmäßigen** Verben musst du dir jedoch gut merken, z.B. *fly: I flew*. Schreibe sie immer zu den Grundformen (auch solchen, die du schon kennst). Nimm dabei für Buchstaben, die in der Grundform **nicht** vorkommen, eine andere Farbe, z.B. *make: I ma**d**e*.

[1] **geocaching** ['dʒiːəʊkæʃɪŋ] Geocaching (eine Art elektronische Schatzsuche)

12 New words ▸ pp. 22–23

Find the English words for the German words in brackets and fill in the gaps.

1 I read a nice little __________ *(Geschichte)* yesterday. **2** I ________ *(liebe)* it! Listen.

3 A long time __________ *(Vor langer Zeit)* there were forests on the __________ *(Küste)* of England.

4 Only ________________ *(Dachse)* and ________ *(wilde)* horses lived there. **5** On a ________ *(kühlen)* summer evening a group of people came to one of the beaches in their boat. **6** They ________ *(fühlten sich)* really hungry. **7** "Let's go ________ *(hinein, in)* the forest and find something to eat," the _________ *(Kopf, Oberhaupt)* of the group said. **8** "But there's no _________ *(Licht)* in the forest. **9** It's too ________ *(dunkel)*," someone said. "Maybe there are bears in there." **10** "Well," the _________ *(Kopf, Oberhaupt)* of the group said, "I can be your __________ *(Führer/in)*. **11** I don't need _________ *(Licht)*. **12** Let me walk ______________________ *(vorne, an vorderster Stelle)*. But you must stay behind me!" **13** At that _______________ *(Moment)* they all heard a terrible __________ *(Lärm)*. **14** They jumped up, ran __________ *(entlang)* the ________ *(Seite)* of their boat and then jumped in. "Quick, let's go!" someone shouted. And they went. – **15** At the beach, one _____________ *(Dachs)* said to the other _______________ *(Dachsen)*, "I __________ *(rate, schätze)* that's it. You can put the megaphone[1] away again, Louis. Let's enjoy the quiet night."

13 Word snail[2]

Finish the English words for the German words (below) in the snail. The first letters can help you. Then put the marked letters in the grass at the bottom of the page and find the secret word.

The secret word: g _ _ _ _ _ p _ _ _ _ _ s

[1] **megaphone** ['megəfəʊn] Megafon [2] **snail** [sneɪl] Schnecke

14 Odd word out

Which word does not fit? Cross it out.

1 head – arm – air – leg

2 start – stop – finish – end

3 budgie – hen – swallow – sheep

4 coast – beach – seaside – ground

5 feel – guess – love – like

6 guide – farmer – badger – teacher

15 Crossword puzzle

Put the simple past forms of the verbs in brackets in the crossword.

Across ▸

1 Yesterday I *(think)*, 'Ruby is really nice.'
4 I *(take)* a lot of photos on holiday last summer.
6 The rain *(stop)* early this morning.
8 We *(do)* great things on holiday last year.
9 My father *(drive)* to work yesterday.
13 We *(live)* in London when I was a little kid.
15 I *(ride)* a black horse on the farm yesterday.
16 I *(see)* your brother two days ago.
19 We *(go)* to the beach a lot on holiday.
20 We *(stay)* at a cottage on the farm last week.

Down ▾

2 The accident *(happen)* a week ago.
3 I *(post)* the letter yesterday.
4 Last week I *(tidy)* my room.
5 I *(borrow)* Lisa's bike last week.
6 Yesterday my mum *(say)* OK.
7 I *(make)* a cake last weekend.
10 We *(close)* our shop last year.
11 Two years ago we *(fly)* to New York.
12 I *(feel)* horrible yesterday.
14 My sister *(move)* to Germany last month.
17 I *(be)* in London last week.
18 I *(lie)* in the sun a lot last summer

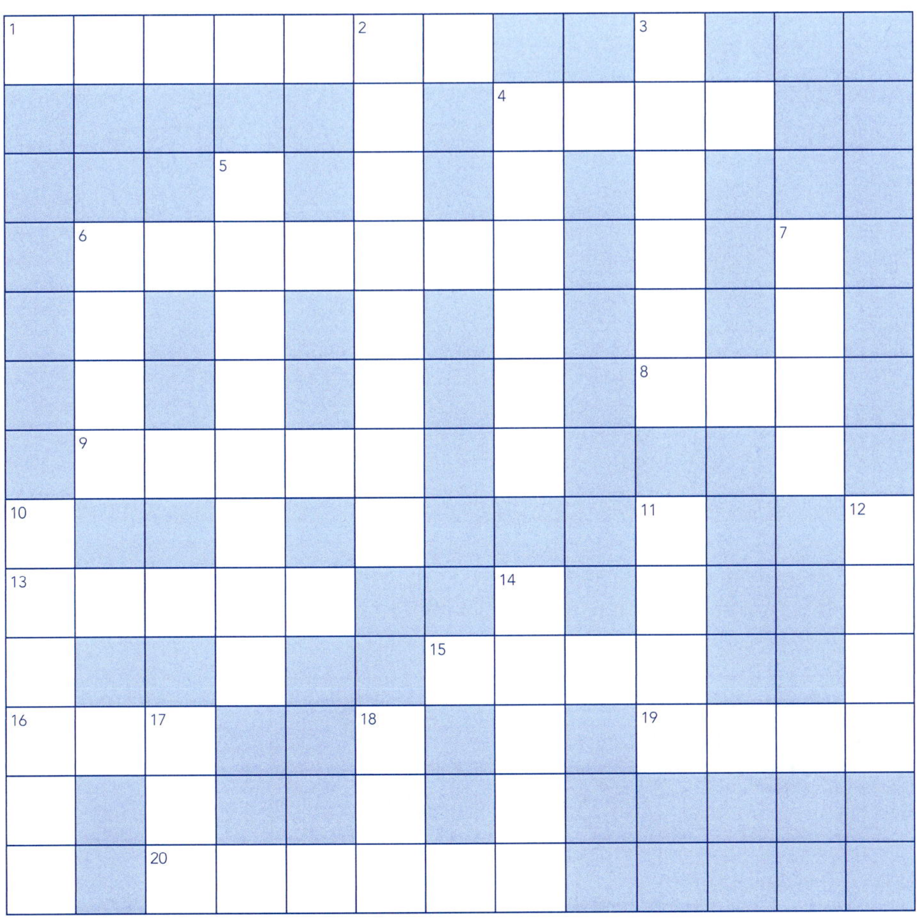

16 New words ▸ pp. 25–27

Find the English words for the German words in brackets and fill in the gaps.

Nick Hi, Sally. **1** Can we have a ______________ *(Gespräch)* with you?

Sally What do you mean?

Anna We're from the school magazine. **2** Can we ______________ *(interviewen)* you?

Sally OK. **3** Are you __________ *(beide)* writing for the school magazine?

Nick Yes, we are. **4** The first question is: Are you ______________ of *(Hast du Angst vor)* our teachers?

Sally No, I'm not. Our teachers are OK. **5** They're **for** us, not ______________ *(gegen)* us.

Anna OK. **6** The next question is: Do you sometimes __________ *(Schläfst du)* in class?

Sally No, of course not! I'm sorry but I must go now. **7** I must ______________ *(meinen Bus erreichen)*.

Nick Oh, OK. Thank you, Sally. Bye.

17 Opposites

Find the opposites. ***Tip:*** *All the opposites have got the letters 'a' or 'o' in them.*

1 (to) love >< (to) __________

2 (to) stop >< (to) __________

3 (to) lie >< (to) __________

4 tomorrow >< __________

5 against >< __________

6 young >< __________

7 first >< __________

8 out of >< __________

9 head >< __________

10 sun >< __________

Lerntipp

Du kennst noch mehr Gegensätze auf Englisch. Fertige ein Memory-Spiel mit *Opposites* an. Immer, wenn du mit neuen Wörtern ein weiteres Gegensatzpaar bilden kannst, erweiterst du das Spiel.

18 New words ▸ pp. 28–29

Find the English words for the German words in brackets and fill in the gaps.

1 My brother is a ________________ *(Rettungsassistent)*. **2** He likes his job because he's never ________ *(gelangweilt)*. Yesterday he told me this story:

3 One quiet night they ____________ *(trugen)* a man on a ______________ *(Tragbahre)* from his house to the ________________ *(Krankenwagen)*. **4** ____________ *(Plötzlich)* there was a very ____________ *(merkwürdiger)* noise. **5** Someone ________ *(rief … an)* the man on his ____________________ *(Handy)*, but the __________________ *(Rettungsassistenten)* didn't know that. **6** Everyone got a terrible __________ *(Schock)* – and the man ____________ *(fiel herunter von)* the ________________ *(Tragbahre)*! **7** He __________ *(landete)* on his ________ *(Rücken)* and didn't move. **8** Then he said in a polite ________ *(Stimme)*, "It's OK. It's ____________ *(nichts)*." **9** My brother said, "________ *(Bleiben Sie)* ________ *(ruhig)*, please, Mr Lewis." **10** And he ________________ *(erklärte)*: "We must ______ *(hochheben)* the ________________ *(Tragbahre)* ______ *(vom … weg)* the ground again now." They were really careful, and everything was OK.

In the hospital my brother talked to Mr Lewis again. Mr Lewis said, "Don't worry, I'm OK.

11 I'm just so ______ *(traurig)*." **12** "Why are you ______ *(traurig)*, Mr Lewis?" my brother asked.

13 The answer: "Because I can't use my ____________________ *(Handy)* in here!"

19 The right word

Put the two words in the right sentences, a) or b).

1 ~~after~~ · for
a) I'm looking *after* Mrs Lee's kids on Saturday.
b) I'm looking ____________ my umbrella. Where is it?

2 again · against
a) We're good! Let's play ____________ the A-Team now.
b) Mum, when can we go to the zoo ____________?

3 noise · voice
a) I can hear Tom's ____________ outside.
b) What's that strange ____________?

4 bored · boring
a) What can I do now? I'm so ____________!
b) I don't like this new game. It's really ____________.

20 Puzzle

Read the German descriptions[1] and write the ten words. What's the mystery word?

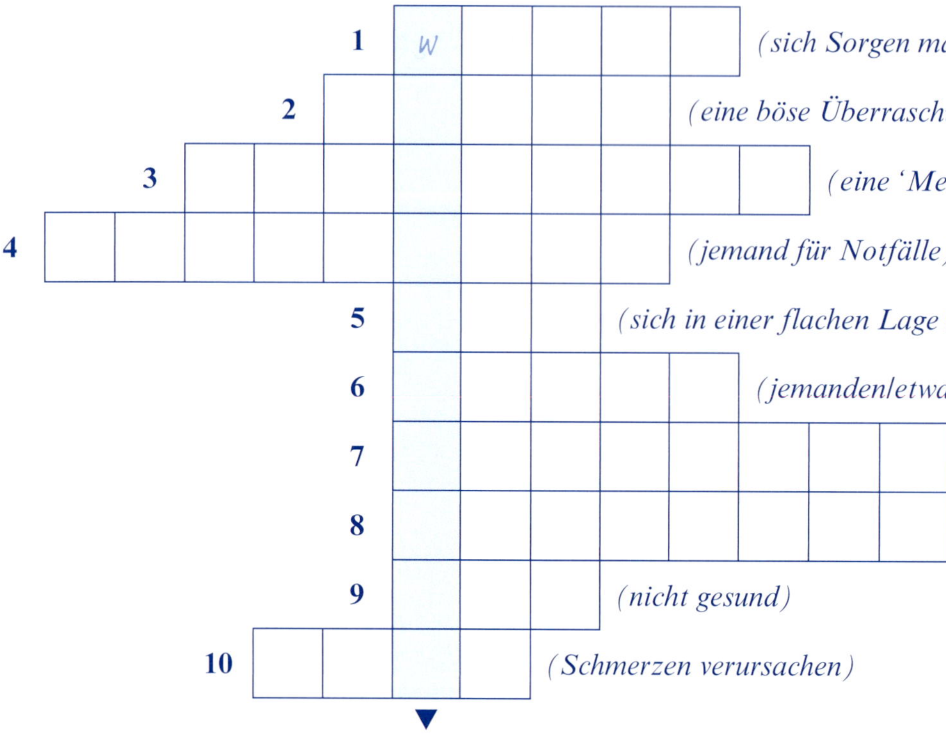

1 W (*sich Sorgen machen*)

2 (*eine böse Überraschung*)

3 (*eine 'Menschentragehilfe'*)

4 (*jemand für Notfälle*)

5 (*sich in einer flachen Lage befinden*)

6 (*jemanden/etwas hochheben und befördern*)

7 (*ein Gebäude mit viel Medizin und vielen Betten*)

8 (*etwas Unvorgesehenes mit schlimmen Folgen*)

9 (*nicht gesund*)

10 (*Schmerzen verursachen*)

▼ (*ein Hilfsmittel für Menschen, die nicht mehr in der Lage sind zu gehen*)

21 One German word = Two English words

Put in the two different English words for the one German word in brackets.

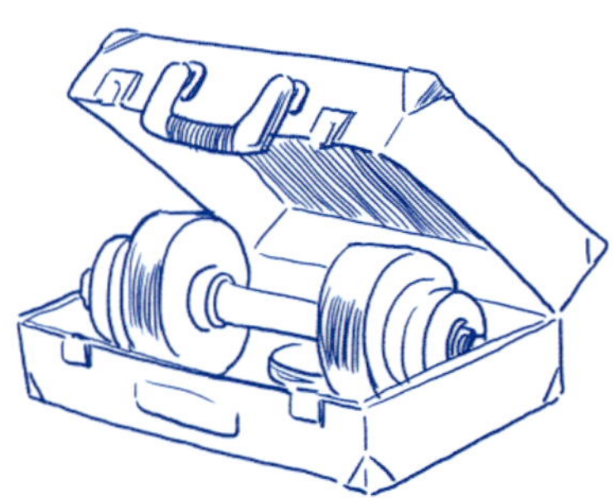

1 (*Seite*) **a)** How do we get to the other side of the stream?

b) Unit 2 starts on p_________ 18 in your book.

2 (*vor*) **a)** The letter from London came two days __________ .

b) We usually let the dog out __________ lunch.

3 (*tragen*) **a)** Ann often __________ blue sweaters and red skirts.

b) I can't __________ this case! What's in it – stones?

4 (*ruhig*) **a)** Sh! Be __________ now, class, and listen to Mary.

b) Can't you sit __________ for one moment, Eric?

5 (*Tasche*) **a)** Put your sport things in your __________ now, please.

b) I found some money in my shirt __________ .

6 (*über*) **a)** Let's talk __________ your summer holidays.

b) The dog jumped __________ the garden fence.

[1] **description** [dɪ'skrɪpʃn] Beschreibung

22 The simple past

a) *Find 15 simple past forms in the puzzle and mark them.*

c	w	b	o	u	g	h	t	s	p	o	k	e	d
t	o	n	d	c	a	u	g	h	t	w	o	r	e
o	n	r	a	n	g	r	t	h	o	u	g	h	t
o	s	i	t	y	e	t	u	f	o	u	n	d	g
k	f	h	e	a	r	d	s	t	d	r	a	n	k
f	e	l	l	w	i	t	o	l	d	e	n	g	s

b) *Put the simple past forms in the table[1] below and add their infinitive form.*

Infinitive	Simple past	Infinitive	Simple past	Infinitive	Simple past
(to) win	won	(to)		(to)	
(to)		(to)		(to)	
(to)		(to)		(to)	
(to)		(to)		(to)	
(to)		(to)		(to)	

c) *Write three short sentences about the past. Use three different simple past forms from* ***b)****.*

(1) Yesterday ______________________________

(2) Last week ______________________________

(3) Last summer ______________________________

d) *Complete this 'simple past poem[2]' with the right simple past forms.*
Can you guess the last verb?

(1) It's 'buy' and 'bought',

(2) And 'catch' and '______________'.

(3) There's 'ring' and '______________',

(4) And 'sing' and '______________'.

(5) I remembered 'keep' and '______________'

(6) 'get' and 'got' – and then I ______________!

[1] **table** ['teɪbl] Tabelle [2] **poem** ['pəʊɪm] Gedicht

23 Missing letters

*Complete the words with the letters **d**, **g**, **h** or **t**.*
***Tip:** The German words are all in the box below.*

1 ba d ger	5 _ roun _	9 li _ _ _
2 bir _	6 _ uess	10 s _ ran _ e
3 co _ _ a _ e	7 _ ui _ e	11 s _ re _ c _ er
4 _ ran _ paren _ s	8 _ ea _	12 _ _ rou _ _

BODEN~~DACHS~~DURCHFÜHRER/INGROẞELTERNHÜTTE
KOPFLICHTMERKWÜRDIGRATENTRAGBAHREVOGEL

24 Word groups

Put the words from the grass into the right flower.

25 Three words

Complete each sentence with three words from the box. Careful! You don't need all the words.

a lot • against • ago • air • best • birds • bored • coast • everyone • first • horses • into • last • ~~lovely~~ • noise • nothing • past • sea • something • strange • stretchers • through • villages • wild

1 Wow – your hair looks really lovely / ____________ / ____________ today!

2 Our holiday in the country was interesting.
I saw a lot of ____________ / ____________ / ____________.

3 I talked to Mike Butler last week.
It was our ____________ / ____________ / ____________ conversation.

4 We often go to Kerry on holiday.
The ____________ / ____________ / ____________ is really lovely there.

5 ____________ / ____________ / ____________ happened last night.
Where were you?

6 Stop! You can't walk ____________ / ____________ / ____________ that wall!

MY LEARNER LOG

Mein Lerntagebuch. Hier notierst du deine Erfahrungen mit dem Wörterlernen.

♥ Meine drei englischen Lieblingswörter aus dieser Unit sind:

____

Diese *Simple past*-Wörter finde ich am lustigsten ☺ :

____

Im Auswendiglernen unregelmäßiger *Simple past*-Formen bin ich …
– sehr gut (ich kann schon mindestens 10). ☐
– gut (ich kann schon mindestens 8). ☐
– befriedigend (ich kann schon mindestens 5). ☐
– noch nicht so gut (ich kann erst ein paar). ☐

1 New words ▸ p. 34

Find the English words for the German words in brackets and fill in the gaps.

Marc I've got a question, Ms Kent. I've got a story for the school magazine. **1** It's about two ____________ *(Elefanten)* in the zoo. Now I need a good picture for the story. Do you know where I can get free pictures?

Ms Kent Yes, I do. **2** The school bought a great ______ *(DVD)* with animal pictures. We can use them for the magazine.

Marc Oh, good. **3** Where's the ________ *(Disk)*?

Ms Kent It's in the school library. Wait, we can look at it together …

Marc Wow. **4** This picture looks fantastic on the ____________ *(Bildschirm)*.

Ms Kent Yes, it does. **5** Now ____________ *(klicke … an)* '__________' *(ausdrucken)* and we can ______________ *(herausfinden)* if it looks good on paper[1], too.

Marc Great. Thanks, Ms Kent.

2 Little words

Complete the sentences with the right 'little' word. You need one of the words for two sentences.

1 Oh look, that's interesting! Can you click ___________ the name at the top, please?

2 I really like this photo of our class. Can I print it ___________, please?

3 My sister can't come to school today. She fell ___________ the garden fence yesterday.

4 I'm looking forward ___________ the summer holidays. We're going to the seaside.

5 We're doing a new project at school. We're finding ___________ about wild animals in Africa.

6 I'm not afraid ___________ big animals, but I'm afraid ___________ mice!

[1] **paper** ['peɪpə] Papier

3 New words ▸ p. 35

Find the English words for the German words in brackets and fill in the gaps.

1 We started a new project in ______________ *(Geschichte)* last week. It's on American presidents. It's a lot of work but it's OK because there are seven kids in our project group. We all work every day. **2** Aya ______________________ *(sucht nach)* information on our subject on many different ________________ *(Websites)*. **3** Benjy looks through old _____________________ *(Tageszeitungen)* and books in the library. **4** Camilla reads _____________________ *(aktuelle)* ________ *(Nachrichten)* on the _______________ *(Internet)*. **5** David __________ *(schickt)* a lot of ______________ *(E-Mails)* to our American partner school. **6** Eden reads _______________ *(Millionen)* ;-) of Twitter _________________ *(Mitteilungen, Nachrichten)* from Washington every day. **7** And Furkan __________ *(tippt)* ____________________ *(alles)* on the school computer. My job? **8** Well, my job is to print out the _____________ *(Ergebnisse)*!

4 Word groups

Find three words for each definition.

books · click on · computers · deer · discs · elephants · ~~e-mails~~ · french · grizzly bears · history · internet · magazines · maths · newspapers · phrases · print · screens · send · sentences · websites · words

1 You use a computer for these:

e-mails, ____

2 You can hold these in your hands and read them:

____

3 These are on many people's desks:

____

4 These are school subjects:

____

5 These are things that you do when you use a computer:

____

6 You use these when you speak or write:

____

7 These are wild animals:

____

5 That's wrong! What's right?

Finish the sentence. Make it short. Use the word in brackets and put the verb in the simple past form.

1 *(pigs)* Marisa didn't find out about elephants on the internet. She found out about pigs.

2 *('Like')* Carlo didn't click on 'Print' on the website. He ______

3 *(postcard)* Lil didn't send me an e-mail from Wales. She ______

4 *(me)* Pavel didn't ring Jim on his mobile. He ______

5 *(excited)* We didn't feel bored at the computer. We ______

6 *(basketball)* I didn't search for football news on the internet. I ______

______

6 Some words rhyme

Find the right rhyme word for each word at the top and draw a line. You don't need all the words!

7 Jumbled sentences

Put the words in the right order.

1 on find can ~~How~~ out we the elephants internet? about

How ______

2 get millions I of 'elephant', I results. in type When

______

3 a lot of I everything, and websites can't the read up-to-date. aren't

______

4 an teacher asked e-mail Yesterday to her. and I sent my

______

8 New words ▸ pp. 36–37

Find the English words for the German words in brackets and fill in the gaps.

1 Last Sunday after lunch my ________________ *(Oma)* said, “Listen. I made a ____________________ *(Vorsatz, Beschluss)* on January 1st. **2** It’s on this ________ *(Karte)*. I don’t want to forget it again. **3** This is it: I'm ________________ *(Ich werde)* walk to town and ____________________ *(mich umschauen in)* the shops every afternoon – if it’s _________ *(warm)* outside and the weather ________________ *(Wettervorhersage)* is good. **4** Who's ________________ *(Wer wird)* come with me?” **5** My little sister said, “Oh please, please, can I come with you, ________________ *(Oma)*? And can Lilly come, too?” **6** ________________ *(Oma)* was very happy. “That’s wonderful, Rosie,” she said. **7** “And of course you can bring your _________ *(Tiger)*.”

9 The weather forecast

Read the weather forecast for the week and put the right day of the week in each box.

13°
1 Sunday

15°
2 ____________

28°
3 ____________

19°
4 ____________

23°
5 ____________

15°
6 ____________

18°
7 ____________

It’s going to be cold on Sunday. That’s tomorrow.
There are going to be lots of clouds on Monday.
It’s going to rain on Tuesday.
But it’s going to get warmer on Wednesday.
The sun is going to come out on Thursday.
It’s going to be warm on Friday.
And it’s going to be really hot on Saturday.
– Great! Can we go to the seaside at the weekend?

10 New words ▸ pp. 38–39

Find the English words for the German words in brackets and fill in the gaps.

Louis Can you help me, Ken? **1** I'm trying to ________________ *(herunterladen)* something from the internet for … eh, my ___________ *(Bericht)* on wild elephants. **2** But there's a __________ *(bedeutendes)* problem: I can't get off this website.

Ken I can't help you with that, sorry. But let me get Mr Hall.

Louis No, not Mr Hall! **3** He doesn't know about ___________________ *(Technik)*, he _____________ *(unterrichtet)* French.

Ken Well, what about Belinda then? **4** She's a _____________ *(Mitglied)* of the computer club. **5** She knows everything about computers, the internet ______________ *(und so weiter)*.

Louis No, not Belinda! Oh, here she is. Hello, Belinda. It's really OK now, I think …

Belinda Let's see. **6** What's the website _____________ *(Adresse)* then? www.bundesliga.com?

Ken What?? **7** That's the German Football ___________ *(Liga)*! What have they got to do with wild elephants?? Oh, Louis. **8** You can't ________________ *(herunterladen)* German football results _______ *(auf …)* the school computer, you know that!

Belinda It's working again.

Louis Oh, great! What's this? www.onlyelephants.com? Oh, OK. Thanks, Belinda.

11 Puzzle 'The internet (and so on)'

Complete the sentences with the right words. What's the mystery word?

1 I've got my own e-mail _ _ _ r _ _ _ now.

2 We haven't got a big _ _ _ _ _ _ _ _ at home. We use a laptop.

3 I found the information on the school's _ _ _ _ _ t _.

4 The colours look different on this _ _ _ e _ _.

5 You can find the photos when you _ _ _ _ _ on 'Pictures' and then on 'Class party'.

6 A computer _ _ _ s _ doesn't really look like the animal, I think.

7 Yesterday I _ _ _ _ _ h _ _ the internet for information on pigs.

8 Can I _ _ _ _ a message to your mobile?

12 New words ▸ pp. 42–43

Find the English words for the German words in brackets and fill in the gaps.

Jill I sent you an e-mail yesterday, but it came back.

Thomas Let me see. **1** You ____________ *(vergaßest)* the letter 'h' in my name. It often happens.

Jill Really? My e-mail address is easier. **2** Look, this is ________ *(meine)*.

Thomas Yes, I know. **3** I've got __________ *(deine)*. You gave it to me last week.

Jill Oh, did I? And what about Jim and Jodie? **4** Did I give you ___________ *(ihre)*, too?

Thomas Your brother's and your sister's e-mail addresses? **5** I think you gave me _______ *(ihre)* – I mean Jodie's. But I don't remember Jim's.

Jill OK, one moment, please. **6** This is _____ *(seine)*. And we've got one address for all the family, too. Let me write it down for you. **7** Look, this is ________ *(unsere)*.

Thomas Well, thanks. I think I've got them all now.

13 Whose is it?

Look at the pictures. Then complete each sentence with the right pronoun.

mine • yours • his • hers • theirs • ours

1 This isn't ______________.
It's ___________________.

2 This isn't ______________.
It's ___________________.

3 That isn't ______________.
It's ___________________.

Hinweis

Pronomen

Vergleiche:

It's …	my book.	your book.	his book.	her book.	their book.	our book.	your book.
It's …	mine.	yours.	his.	hers.	theirs.	ours.	yours.

Aufgepasst: Kein Apostroph!

14 New words ▸ pp. 44–45

Find the English words for the German words in brackets and fill in the gaps.

Jessica That was a nice afternoon. **1** But it's ________ *(es wird)* late. I'm going home now.

Nishi OK. **2** Oh, I forgot: I ______ *(bekam)* an e-mail from my brother in America yesterday. Wait, I can show you … **3** Let's ________________ *(einschalten)* the light, it's so dark in here. **4** Do you ________ *(Magst du)* a _________ *(Glas)* of water?

Jessica No, thanks.

Nishi OK. Now, here's his mail. **5** ______________________________ *(Ich bin interessiert an)* sport and my brother knows that, of course. **6** He __________ *(schrieb)* about _______________ *(Softball)*. **7** A lot of the girls at his ____________________ *(Oberschule)* play it.

Jessica **8** _______________ *(Softball)*? Is that a joke?

Nishi **9** No, it's a _____________ *(ernstes)* game in America. And the best thing is: I'm going to visit him and play with them.

Jessica **10** Really? ______ *(Wahnsinn)*!

15 Opposites

Read both sentences, a) and b). Then complete the sentences with opposites.

1 a) Eileen is my father's mother. She's my grandma.

b) John is Eileen's husband. He's my ____________ .

2 a) Ms Miller ____________ English at Hill School. She's a teacher.

b) Jake ____________ English at Hill School. He's a pupil.

3 a) 'Fun first!' is a very ____________ TV programme. The presenter tells lots of jokes.

b) 'Today' is a very ____________ TV programme. The presenter tells us the news of the day.

4 a) It's a ____________ evening. Let's sit outside.

b) It's a ____________ evening. I'm going to wear a sweater.

5 a) I'm ________________ in sport. I watch a lot of football on TV.

b) I'm ________________ with sport. I never watch it on TV. I watch films.

6 a) I read all the books, I answered all the questions – I did ____________ for the quiz. I'm going to win!

b) I didn't read the books or the questions – I did ____________ for the quiz. I'm not going to win.

16 The weather forecast

Complete the sentences

1 It's going to be cool on Saturday. 

2 Then the weather is going to get worse. On Sunday there are going to be lots of ____________ . 

3 The worst day is going to be Monday. Take an umbrella because it's going to ________ . 

4 On Tuesday it's going to get better again. It's going to be ____________ than on Monday. 

5 And on Wednesday the ______ is going to come out and it's going to be really ______ . 

17 The wrong word

*Cross out the word that does **not** belong in the sentence. Then write the letter (after the ▸) below. Add three more letters and find the mystery word.*

1	He	a) ~~carries~~ ▸ D	b) fancies ▸ P	c) hates ▸ N	d) likes ▸ K	Corinna.
2	I	a) left ▸ A	b) found ▸ I	c) bought ▸ O	d) put ▸ U	my bag on the floor.
3	I	a) forgot ▸ C	b) found out ▸ R	c) looked round ▸ F	d) remembered ▸ S	his birthday.
4	I	a) got ▸ Y	b) taught ▸ E	c) sent ▸ S	d) wrote ▸ I	a mail.
5	I	a) downloaded ▸ L	b) clicked on ▸ P	c) searched for ▸ M	d) switched on ▸ U	a photo.
6	It's	a) mine. ▸ T	b) it's. ▸ W	c) ours. ▸ C	d) yours. ▸ W	

			D					
6	2		1	4		3	5	

!

18 Questions and answers

Complete each question with the right question word from the box.
Match the questions (1–6) with the answers (a–f). Draw lines.

How? • What? • When? • Where? • Who? • Why?

1 ________ is your New Year resolution?
2 ________ told you about this website?
3 ________ did you send Bonnie the message?
4 ________ did you download the results?
5 ________ can I find the school's website?
6 ________ did you print out the report?

a) On Sunday.
b) I just clicked on 'download'.
c) I'm going to help my grandma every Saturday.
d) A member of the computer club.
e) I thought you'd like to take it with you.
f) Well, the address is www.school…

19 The fourth[1] word

Find the fourth word and fill it in. ***Tip:*** *The words are all on the right – but the letters and the words are in the wrong order.*

1 boys – girls | baseball – softball

2 table – wood | window – ____________

3 my – your | mine – ____________

4 type – typed | fancy – ____________

5 forgot – remembered | searched – ____________

6 website – internet | news – ____________

7 league – teams | club – ____________

8 teach – taught | send – ____________

spreanwep
donuf
nest
~~blastfol~~
slags
defanic
bremsem
rusyo

20 Making new words

How many new words can you make from the word 'everything'? You can use only the letters in the word, but you can use the letters more than once[2].

e v e r y t h i n g

get, right, try, ____________

____

____

MY LEARNER LOG

Mein Lerntagebuch. Hier notierst du deine Erfahrungen mit dem Wörterlernen.

♥ Meine drei englischen Lieblingswörter aus dieser Unit sind:

____

Diese Wörter aus der Unit kann ich mir besonders schlecht merken:

____

Zum Wörterlernen mache ich besonders gern:

Kreuzworträtsel ☐ andere Rätsel ☐ Vokabelnetze ☐ Ausspracheübungen (wie Ex. 6) ☐

'Jumbled sentences'-Übungen (wie Ex. 7) ☐ 'The fourth word'-Übungen (wie Ex. 19) ☐

oder: ____________

[1] **fourth** [fɔːθ] vierte/r/s [2] **once** [wʌns] einmal

1 New words ▸ p. 48

Find the English words for the German words in brackets and fill in the gaps.

Hi Mum and Dad,

Yesterday was a very strange day here in Britain. In the morning the teacher at school told us about a terrorist[1]. **1** This man tried to ____________ *(in die Luft jagen)* the English king! I didn't understand – the king? I thought they had a queen … The other children thought it was all very exciting. **2** In the afternoon the children made a ____________ *(besondere)* scarecrow[2].

3 They called it the '_______' *(Typen, Burschen)*. **4** They also made plans to _________ *(anzünden)* a ________ *(Feuer)* later. Good, I thought, because it's really cold here at the moment.

Then suddenly, in the evening, there was a lot of noise. Oh no, I thought, the terrorists are here! But the children laughed and ran outside. **5** I followed them and we saw some great ___________________ *(Feuerwerk)*. **6** Then the children took the '______' *(Typen, Burschen)* to the park. There were lots of people in the park. **7** They _____ *(zündeten … an)* a _____________ *(Freudenfeuer, Guy-Fawkes-Feuer)*. **8** And then they __________ *(verbrannten)* someone on the _______ *(Feuer)*!

9 No, not really: it was the '_______' *(Typ, Bursche)*. Britain is strange!

I'm looking forward to Florida (and you!) in December.

Love, Selina

2 What happened?

Complete the sentences with the right verb in the simple past form.
*(**Tip:** If you need help, look at exercise 1.)*
Then add the verb in the infinitive.

1 The teacher t o l d the children a story. (to t e l l)

2 The children _ _ _ _ a 'guy'. (to _ _ _ _)

3 In the evening the children _ _ _ the fireworks. (to _ _ _)

4 They _ _ _ _ the 'guy' to the park. (to _ _ _ _)

5 The people in the park _ _ _ a bonfire. (to _ _ _ _ _)

6 They _ _ _ _ _ the 'guy' on the fire. (to _ _ _ _)

[1] **terrorist** ['terərɪst] Terrorist/in [2] **scarecrow** ['skeəkrəʊ] Vogelscheuche

3 New words ▸ p. 49

Find the English words for the German words in brackets and fill in the gaps.

Hi Lalit,

Thanks for your mail. You want to come to Germany, that's great! But at the end of October?? **1** Don't be a ________ *(Narr, Dummkopf)*. **2** ______________ (Herbst) in Bavaria is ________ *(etwas, ein wenig)* boring. **3** The big _______________ *(Fest, Festival)* in Munich (the famous 'Oktoberfest') is over[1]. There's no Bonfire Night here. **4** We haven't got many ___________ *(Hindu)* _______________ *(Tempel, Kultstätten)* for Diwali … Here's an idea: Why don't you come in the week before Christmas? The Christmas markets in Germany are fantastic! **5** You can buy Christmas presents for your family, like nice ______________ *(Kerzen)* or German sweets. **6** Oh, now I've got _______________ *(eine andere, noch eine)* idea: Come for 'Fasching'! Do you know 'Fasching'? **7** People wear silly things and have a lot of ______ *(Spaß)*. **8** Last year I was a ____________ *(Spinne)* ☺ I'm going to send you a photo later. Yes, please come for 'Fasching'. **9** ______________ *(Es macht Spaß)*!

Love, Pia

4 Puzzle 'Definitions'

Complete each definition with a word from the candles and give the right word for the definition. Complete the definition for the mystery word with words from the candles.

1 It ___________ and gives light: _ _ _ _ _ _

2 To be on ___________: _ _ _ _

3 A special day (or days) in the year when people ___________ working: _ _ _ _ _ _ _ _

4 Another word for a ___________: _ _ _

5 It's where Hindus ___________ together at Diwali: _ _ _ _ _ _

6 A special, ___________ fire outside: _ _ _ _ _ _ _

➜ _ _ _ _ _ _ is the time _______________ the summer and _______________ Christmas.

[1] **over** ['əʊvə] vorbei

5 New words ▸ pp. 50–51

Find the English words for the German words in brackets and fill in the gaps.

Tina Pavel, it's terrible! **1** We ________ *(verloren)* the football game today.

2 That means we won't win the League _______ *(Pokal)*.

Pavel Don't be sad. **3** Let's go to the school quiz ________________ *(heute Abend)*.

4 We can win a ___________ *(Preis, Gewinn)* there, too.

Tina Really? How?

Pavel **5** We're just going to give _________ *(ein paar)* right answers and win!

Tina **6** And what's the ___________ *(Preis, Gewinn)*?

Pavel **7** It's a ________ of *(Paar)* football shoes …

6 The spider

It can't be 'spider'! What's the right word in each sentence? The letters are all in the box.

A A A A B B B B C E E E E E F F F F H I K L L L L M N O O O O O O P R R S T T T

1 The school's ~~spider~~ team lost again last week. football

2 Don't be a spider! Don't stay in the house on Bonfire Night. __________________

3 Would you like a cup of tea with your spider this morning? __________________

4 We didn't have a spider last November because it rained. __________________

5 We're Hindus. We sometimes go to the spider and light some candles. __________________

6 My family had a lot of fun on the spider last summer. __________________

7 The right word

Underline the word that belongs in the sentence. Cross out the other word.

1 I'm sorry. I ate *a lot of* / *much crisps* because I was so hungry.

2 Come in, little brother. There are *many* / *no* spiders in your bedroom now.

3 The festival was great. I saw *a few* / *a bit* people from school there.

4 We can't go to the beach. The weather is *much* / *very* bad this week.

5 Poor Jill! She's *a lot of* / *a bit* sad because she lost her mobile yesterday.

6 What can I do? I can't buy a new mobile because I haven't got *much* / *some* money.

8 New words
▸ pp. 52–53

Find the English words for the German words in brackets and fill in the gaps.

Mel **1** Let's play 'The ________ *(Komplott, Verschwörung)* against the queen', OK? **2** Let's go down to the ____________ *(Keller)*. **3** You're a ______________ *(Verschwörerin)* and I'm a ______________ *(Soldatin)*. OK, Cora? **4** This box is a ____________ *(Fass)* full of ____________________ *(Schießpulver)*. **5** The ______________ *(Verschwörerin)* – you – ______________ *(hat gegraben)* a ____________ *(Tunnel)* from outside into the ____________ *(Keller)*. **6** Now she's coming through the tunnel with the ____________ *(Fass)*. **7** Now the ______________ *(Soldatin)* – me – can hear something. **8** I say 'Dear _______ *(Gott)*, what's that? **9** My ___________ *(Keller)* isn't ___________ *(leer)*! **10** Is there a _______________ *(Katholikin)* in here? **11** Is she bringing the queen ____________________ *(Schießpulver)* and __________ *(Tod)*?' **12** Now the ______________ *(Verschwörerin)* – you, Cora – has a shock, and she __________ *(lässt fallen)* the ____________ *(Fass)*. **13** I jump ____________ *(über, hinüber)* the room and – ow!!

Cora **14** _________________________________ *(Was ist los)*, Mel?

Mel I think I've hurt my leg …

9 What do you say?

Match the people and situations on the left (1–6) with the statements on the right (a–f). Draw lines.

1 You think your friend is going to do something stupid.
2 You're at a great party. You're really enjoying it.
3 Your friend is coming to see you. She looks sad.
4 You're at a party. You don't know one of the boys.
5 You're a police officer. A criminal is standing in front of you.
6 Your friend is going to a party. You hope he's going to enjoy it.

a) Who's that guy?
b) Don't be a fool!
c) This is fun!
d) Drop the gun!
e) Have fun!
f) What's the matter?

10 Odd word out

Which word does not fit? Cross it out.

1 Christmas – ~~May~~ – Diwali – Bonfire Night – Easter
2 fireworks – candle – fire – temple – bonfire
3 tunnel – cellar – kitchen – bedroom – hall
4 leave – drive – lose – drop – forget
5 barrel – bottle – cup – glass – plot
6 soldier – plotter – spider – guy – fool

11 The right word in English and German

Find the word with the jumbled letters in each sentence and cross it out. Write it correctly and give the German word for it, too.

1 Let's take this path. It goes ~~grohthu~~ the forest to the river. through – durch

2 Tea is ready, children. Come noit the house now, please. ______

3 We're looking for our dog. She smelled something and then ran fof. ______

4 Let's move the glasses toon the higher shelf. Karen is bringing her little sister. ______

5 Can we swim scraso the river? There's a nice little beach on the other side. ______

6 We walked gloan that boring road for about two miles! ______

12 Missing letters

*Put in the letters **a**, **e**, **i**, **o**, **u** or **y**. **Tip:** All the words are new in Unit 4.*

1 m _ t t _ r

2 c _ l l _ r

3 b _ r r _ l

4 s _ l d _ _ r

5 d _ _ t h

6 _ m p t _

7 t _ m p l _

8 c _ n d l _

9 C _ t h _ l _ c

10 s p r _ n g

11 t _ n _ g h t

12 g _ n p _ w d _ r

13 The right verb

Complete the sentences with the right past participle form from the box. Careful! You don't need all the verbs.

bought • caught • drunk • eaten • fallen • forgotten • gone • lain • lit • ridden • thought • worn

1 Oh no! Benny has ______ off the tree. Quick, call Dad!

2 Oh no! I've ______ the wrong way. Where am I?

3 Oh no! The children have ______ the fire. Look!

4 Oh no! We've ______ to do our homework! Quick, let's do it now.

5 Oh no! You've ______ the wrong crisps, Mum! We don't like these.

6 Oh no! The dog has ______ all our sausages! What are we going to do now?

Lerntipp

Du findest die *past participle*-Formen der unregelmäßigen Verben in der Liste „Irregular verbs" (GO AHEAD 6, S.152–153) in der dritten Spalte. Unten auf S.153 findest du außerdem ein paar Tipps dafür, wie du dir die beiden Formen der unregelmäßigen Verben besser merken kannst. In welche der dort genannten Kategorien (*Chicken verbs* etc.) kannst du die unregelmäßigen Verben *drink* und *think* einordnen? Aufpassen: Es sind zwei verschiedene!

14 New words ▸ pp. 56–57

Find the English words for the German words in brackets and fill in the gaps.

Mum **1** Kira, ______________________________ *(hast du den Tisch gedeckt)* ______ *(schon)*?

Kira No, I haven't, Mum. **2** I've ________ *(gerade)* started. But there's a problem: There aren't ______________ *(genug)* glasses.

Julian Oh, sorry. **3** ______________________________ *(Ich habe noch nicht abgespült)*.

Kira **4** But you've ______________ *(schon)* read all your new _____________ *(Comics)*, haven't you, Julian?

Julian Sh, sister. Don't tell Mum, OK? **5** And don't tell her about the money from you for the _______________ *(Konzert-)* tickets, OK?

Kira Money? Tickets? What are you talking about? **6** _________________________ *(Ich habe nicht geliehen)* you ______ *(irgendwelches)* money.

Julian No, but you're going to. … Aren't you?

15 Puzzle

Write the English words in the puzzle and find the mystery word in the middle.
Write the German word for number 6 in the box on the right.

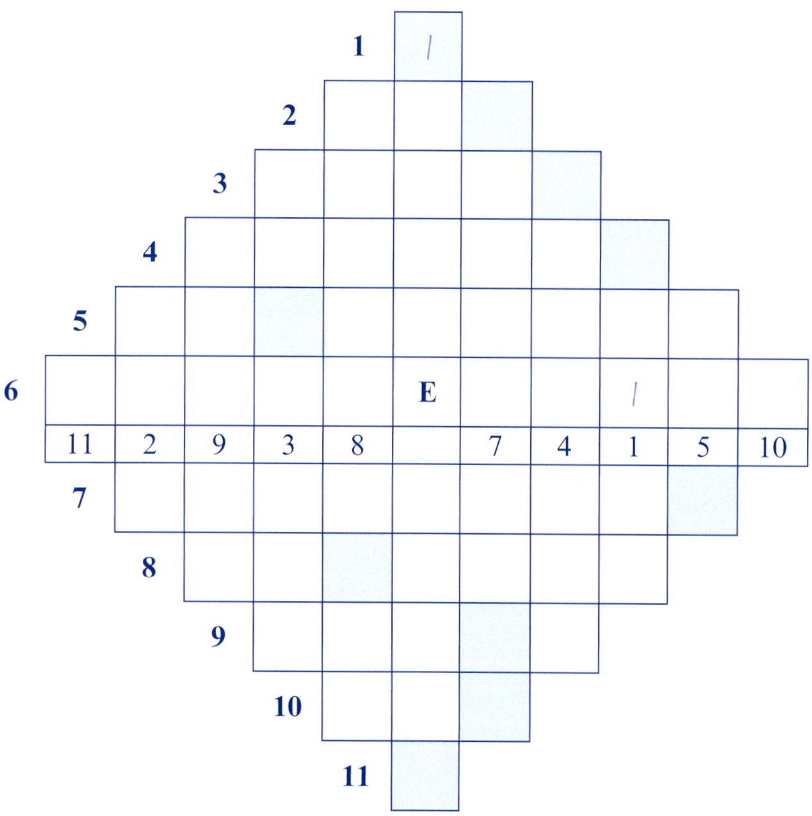

1 ich
2 Spaß
3 Preis, Gewinn
4 Konzert
5 Schießpulver
6 ______________________
7 Feuerwerk
8 schon
9 leer
10 graben
11 ich

16 New words ▸ pp. 58–59

Find the English words for the German words in brackets and fill in the gaps.

1 We went to an amusement park[1] in the __________ *(Winter-)* holidays. **2** At the __________ *(Eingang)* I bought some __________ *(Süßigkeiten)*. **3** My mum __________ *(warnte)* me: "These are very __________ *(hart, zäh)*. **4** Why don't you buy some __________ *(weiche)* __________ *(Süßigkeiten)*?" But it was too late. We went into the park. **5** There was a beautiful lake with some __________ *(Enten)* on it. **6** __________ *(Oberhalb, Über)* the lake was a fantastic __________ *(Schloss, Burg)*. **7** It looked just like the __________ *(Schlösser, Burgen)* in my old picture books. **8** "Mum, the __________ *(Enten)* look hungry. Let's feed them," I said. **9** __________ *(Ich war froh)* I had the __________ *(Süßigkeiten)* because I was hungry, too. **10** But my mum __________ *(lachte über)* me. **11** "You can't give those __________ *(Süßigkeiten)* to the poor __________ *(Enten)*. They can't eat them," she said. At that moment we heard a funny noise. "What's that, Mum?" I asked. She didn't know. **12** __________ *(Vor)* us were some soldiers in funny uniforms. **13** When they heard the __________ *(Signal)*, they all __________ *(feuerten)* their guns in the air – __________ *(peng)*! What a shock! Suddenly I felt a bit strange. **14** I put the __________ *(Süßigkeiten)* back in my pocket. My mum said, "What's the matter? **15** Have you lost your __________ *(Appetit)*? **16** Do we need a __________ *(Arzt/Ärztin)*?" I said, "Thanks, Mum. I'm fine. Can we just go to the rides now, please?"

17 Picture puzzle

Look at the picture and find seven more things.

barrel

____

____

____

____

____

____

____

[1] **amusement park** [əˈmjuːzmənt pɑːk] Vergnügungspark

18 Word ladder

Go up the ladder step by step.
Change (only) one letter each time.

9 You can ride a horse or a ★ .

8 I hate winter, but I really ★ summer.

7 I ★ in Bristol.

6 the opposite of 'take'

5 go – went / give – ★

4 I'm bored. – Why don't we play a ★ ?

3 the opposite of 'different'

2 Can I have ★ water, please?

1 I'm tired. Let's go ★ .

19 Fire!

Complete the sentences with two or three words/phrases from the box.

(to) blow up • bonfires • burn • candles • (to) fire • fire • gun • gunpowder • (to) light • lit

1 Every day at one o'clock they ________________ a ________________ at the castle in Edinburgh.

2 Last winter we often ________________ a ________________ in our living-room in the evenings.
It was nice and warm.

3 ________________ are very popular in the winter. People like to watch them ________________ .

4 On the fifth of November people all over Britain ________________ ________________ .

5 The plotters had lots of ________________, but they didn't ________________ the Parliament.

20 Word groups

Complete each group of words with the right word.

1 swallow – hen – d u c k

2 summer – autumn – w _ _ _ _ r

3 on – over – a _ _ _ e

4 chocolate – cake – s _ _ _ _ s

5 music – band – c _ _ _ _ _ t

6 tower – palace – c _ _ _ _ e

21 New words ▸ pp. 62–63

Find the English words for the German words in brackets and fill in the gaps.

Lou Hi, Emily. What are you doing?

Emily **1** ______________________ *(Wir laden, beladen gerade)* the car for our ________ *(Reise)* to London.

Lou London? You're lucky! **2** Are you going to do a lot of ______________________ *(Besichtigungen)*?

Emily Yes, of course. And we don't need a guide or a bus tour for that.

Lou Why not? Because you've got your smartphones?

Emily No, because my cousin Jack is going to show us the sights. And Jack knows everything. **3** He's an ______________________ *(Enzyklopädie)* on legs!

22 Crossword puzzle 'Travelling'

Read the clues[1] and put the English words in the crossword.

Across ▸
- **3** you take it through a city, usually as a group
- **4** to be in a place for some time and not move away
- **5** what tourists do in a city
- **7** another word for 3 *down*
- **8** a person that explains things as a job
- **9** to move around

Down ▾
- **1** a thing for your things
- **2** a thing that gives an answer to the question 'where?'
- **3** another word for 7 *across*
- **4** what you see in a city (when you do 5 *across*)
- **6** a person that is on holiday in another city or country

[1] **clue** [klu:] Hinweis

23 Past participles

a) *Find the six past participles in the box and mark them.*

lay • drank • written • fell • went • spoken • flew • wore •
seen • took • been • ate • rung • drove • done • forgot

b) *Write the past participles from a) in this table[1] and add the other forms.*

Infinitive	Simple past	Past participle	German
(to) write	wrote	written	schreiben
(to)			
(to)			
(to)			
(to)			
(to)			

c) *Write three short sentences. Use three different past participles from b).*

(1) Have you ______________________________ yet?

(2) I've just ______________________________ .

(3) Max hasn't ______________________________ yet.

24 Puzzle 'Opposites and synonyms'

Find the right >< opposites and >> synonyms and get the mystery past participle.

1 (to) be glad >< (to) be s a d

2 tough >< _ _ _ _

3 (to) borrow >< (to) _ _ _ _

4 guy >> _ _ _

5 (to) be happy >> (to) be _ _ _ _

6 life >< _ _ _ _ _

7 a bit >< _ _ _ _

8 journey >> _ _ _ _

9 empty >< _ _ _ _

10 hard >> _ _ _ _ _

The mystery past participle:

9	2	7	5	10	6	8	3	4

[1] **table** ['teɪbl] Tabelle

25 Network

*Make a word network for 'The year'. Think of the weather, festivals, nature[1], …
You can use some of the new words below, too.*

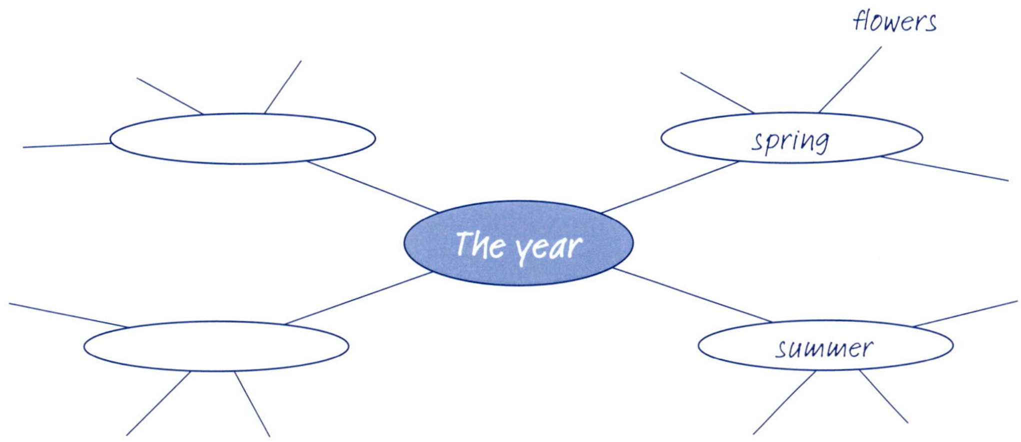

Some useful extra words:
egg [eg] Ei; **carnival** ['kɑːnɪvl] Karneval, Fasching; **costume** ['kɒstjuːm] Kostüm; **harvest** ['hɑːvɪst] Ernte; **leaf/leaves** [liːf, liːvz] Blatt/Blätter; (to) **ski** [skiː] Ski fahren; (to) **snow** [snəʊ] schneien, Schnee

MY LEARNER LOG

Mein Lerntagebuch. Hier notierst du deine Erfahrungen mit dem Wörterlernen.

♥ Meine drei englischen Lieblingswörter aus dieser Unit sind:

____

Diese Reihen unregelmäßiger Verbformen (wie *go – went – gone*) finde ich …

besonders lustig ☺ : ______________________________

besonders seltsam 😐 : ______________________________

besonders schwierig ☹ : ______________________________

Im Auswendiglernen unregelmäßiger Verbformen (mit allen drei Formen!) bin ich …

– sehr gut (ich kann schon mindestens 10). ☐

– gut (ich kann schon mindestens 8). ☐

– befriedigend (ich kann schon mindestens 5). ☐

– noch nicht so gut (ich kann erst ein paar). ☐

[1] **nature** ['neɪtʃə] die Natur

1 New words ▸ p. 64

Find the English words for the German words in brackets and fill in the gaps.

Hi Nick, Can you help me, please? It's my mum's birthday next month and I want to give her a special present. **1** I found an English ______________ *(Fabrik)* on the internet. **2** They make _______ *(Marmelade, Konfitüre)* and ___________ *(Honig)*. **3** They also ______________ *(liefern)* to Germany. **4** It's ____ *(so)* easy! **5** But the problem is: I can't find orange _______ *(Marmelade, Konfitüre)* on their website. My mum loves oranges! Can you look on their website for me, please? It's www.englishjam… Love, Jonas

6 Hi Jonas, That's easy: It's orange _____________________ *(Marmelade aus Zitrusfrüchten)*, not _______ *(Marmelade, Konfitüre)*! Look here: www.englishjam… **7** It's good that they ______________ *(liefern)* it to Germany. But be careful: It's going to get expensive! Love, Nick

2 Definitions

a) *Find the word for the definitions.*

1 A place where a lot of doctors help people: h o s p i t a l
2 To take something to a place where it must go: _ _ _ i _ _ _
3 A place where people work to make things: _ _ _ t _ _ _
4 To make a hole in the ground: _ i _
5 A place where people go to buy food and drinks: _ _ _ _ _ m _ _ _ _ _
6 To put parts together to make something (like a house): _ _ i _ _

b) *Choose the right word from a) to complete the sentences. Careful: Use the right form of the word.*

1 Sarah is a postwoman. She ____________________ hundreds of letters every day.
2 Eric had an accident. The paramedics took him to the hospital.
3 Oh no! Rusty has ____________________ a big hole in the garden again!
4 Can you see the red house over there? My cousin helped to ____________________ it.
5 My father works in a big car ____________________. They make the best cars in the world!
6 We need a lot of things for our meal tonight. – No problem! I can go to the ____________________.

3 New words ▸ p. 65

Find the English words for the German words in brackets and fill in the gaps.

1 I haven't got enough ______________ *(Kleidung)*! **2** I can't buy new things because I don't ________ *(verdiene)* enough money in the ____________ *(Büro)*. **3** Sometimes I go to a _____________ *(Markt)* in East London. **4** They ______ *(verkaufen)* cheap, _________ *(saubere)* _____________ *(Kleidung)* there. **5** And at the weekends I try to ________ *(verdienen)* some _________ *(zusätzliches)* money – I'm a taxi ____________ *(Fahrer/in)* on Sundays. **6** Last weekend I borrowed some _____________ *(Kleidung)* from my cousins. **7** They ________ *(halten, behalten)* a lot of old things in their large wardrobe. They're so old, they're up-to-date again! Then, on Sunday, a woman wanted a taxi because her dog was ill. **8** She thought the dog needed a ______ *(Tierarzt/-ärztin)*. But when I drove along a busy road and another dog was in the car next to us, her dog jumped up and over the seat onto my legs! I was lucky. I didn't have an accident. **9** But the dog was really _________ *(schmutzig)*, and my cousins' _____________ *(Kleidung)* didn't look good. **10** I tried, but I ______________________________________ *(brachte sie nicht sauber)*. What am I going to do now?

4 Verb search

Find the right verb in the puzzle to finish each phrase.

1 help people
2 ____________ at a joke
3 ____________ clean
4 ____________ clothes
5 ____________ cows
6 ____________ money
7 ____________ a hole
8 ____________ post
9 ____________ the car
10 ____________ the gun
11 ____________ the table
12 ____________ the text

b	u	x	l	a	y	m	y	e	n
l	k	e	e	p	e	d	t	a	n
u	r	d	e	l	i	v	e	r	y
m	e	f	s	g	r	i	w	n	p
c	h	i	d	i	g	l	s	b	y
h	t	r	i	n	j	l	o	a	d
e	b	e	l	f	u	d	g	m	c
l	a	u	g	h	v	i	e	x	o
p	o	a	e	h	s	k	t	y	p
t	h	s	e	l	l	z	d	g	y

5 New words ▸ p. 66

Find the English words for the German words in brackets and fill in the gaps.

Lianne This is an interesting advertisement. Look, Paula!

1 Do you need ________ *(Hilfe)*? **2** Get a __________ *(Roboter)*!

3 A __________ *(Roboter)* can help you with all the things that ________ *(dauern, in Anspruch nehmen)* too much time in your life.

★ It can help you in the kitchen: **4** It can put the __________ *(Butter)* on your __________ *(Brot)*. **5** It can open your ________ *(Büchsen, Dosen)* of __________ *(Bohnen)* for you.

★ It can help you with your clothes and other things: It keeps everything clean.

★ **6** It can help you to ______________ *(vorzubereiten, dich fertig zu machen)* in the mornings: **7** It can find your bag and your __________ *(Geldbeutel)*. **8** It can help you to put your ________ *(Mantel)* on.

9 In the __________ *(Zukunft)*, everyone ______ *(wird)* have a __________ *(Roboter)*!

Paula **10** Yes, it's interesting – but I don't have to wait _________ *(bis)* the __________ *(Zukunft)*. I've got Mum and Dad. They do all that for me!

6 Take three

Make groups of three words. Take one from each robot and another word from exercise 5.

1 ice-cream, yoghurt, butter

2 ____________________

3 ____________________

4 ____________________

5 ____________________

6 ____________________

7 New words ▸ pp. 68–69

Find the English words for the German words in brackets and fill in the gaps.

Mehdi **1** My Thinkobot is going to ___________ *(kommt … an)* ________ *(bald)*. Who needs the future? **2** The ______________ *(Gegenwart)* is exciting enough!

Mariam What are you talking about, Mehdi? What's a Thinkobot?

Mehdi A Thinkobot is like a robot. **3** It's going to help me with my homework and my _________ *(Tests, Schulaufgaben)*.

Mariam What? **4** Robots like that don't _________ *(existieren, vorhanden sein)*!

Mehdi Yes, they do. I found an internet company. **5** They sell Thinkobots for a ________ *(fairen, gerechten)* _________ *(Preis)*. **6** They ________ *(sparen)* a lot of money because Thinkobots are like robots, but ______________ *(ohne)* the legs. A Thinkobot can think, but it can't move.

Mariam Ah. **7** It won't walk into the kitchen and help you with the ________________ *(Kartoffeln)*?

Mehdi No, of course not.

Mariam **8** And it won't come into my room and _________ *(stehlen)* my sweets for you?

Mehdi What? No!

Mariam It can't walk then. **9** _____________________ *(Schade)*. It's very much like a computer, isn't it?

Mehdi **10** You're right – _________ *(verflucht, verdammt)*!

8 The fourth[1] word

Find the fourth word.
Tip: *The words are all on the right – but the letters and words are in the wrong order.*

1	(to) buy – (to) sell	(to) arrive – (to) *leave*
2	funny – sad	clean – ________________
3	take – I've taken	steal – I've ________________
4	factory – factories	potato – ________________
5	doctor – people	vet – ________________
6	office – desk	factory – ________________
7	today – yesterday	present – ________________
8	(to) rain – rain	(to) help – ________________

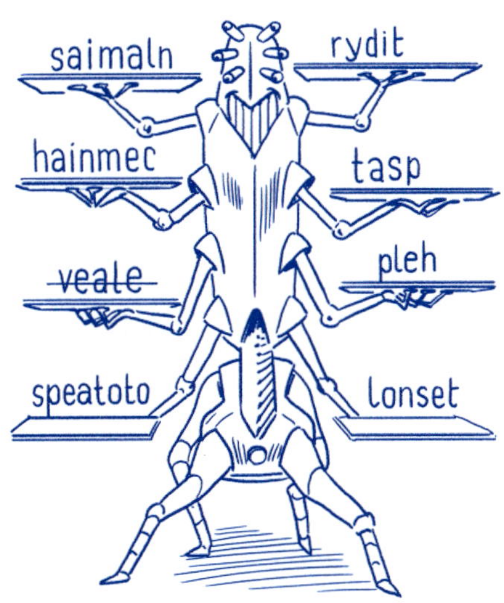

[1] **fourth** [fɔːθ] vierte/r/s

9 Only two

Only two of the three words make a good sentence. Cross out the word that doesn't belong.

1 I like breakfast. Bread with *honey* / *jam* / ~~*tin*~~ is my favourite food!

2 I'm not going to buy the green sweater. I want to *keep* / *save* / *take* my pocket money.

3 Someone has *cleaned* / *found* / *stolen* my purse, but there was no money in it.

4 My grandma always said that this meal is best *until* / *with* / *without* the extra butter.

5 That's strange. The Taylors' son has *arrived* / *left* / *lent* without a case.

6 I like this meal, but I'm not a big fan of *beans* / *clothes* / *potatoes*.

10 Word web

Write the English words for the German words below in the web. They all begin with s-.

1 finanziell unterstützen
2 weich, zart
3 Süßigkeiten
4 stehlen
5 Frühling
6 sparen
7 Soldat/in
8 bald
9 verkaufen
10 so
11 Signal
12 Spinne

11 Pronunciation

Which is the right sound at the end of these pairs of words? Is it [s] *or* [z]*? Put the words into German.*

		[s]	[z]			[s]	[z]	
1	place	✔		–	plays		✔	*Ort, Platz – spielt*
2	phrase			–	race			
3	ice			–	eyes			
4	price			–	prize			
5	size			–	mice			
6	sides			–	sights			
7	sits			–	kids			

12 New words ▸ pp. 72–73

Find the English words for the German words in brackets and fill in the gaps.

Harry **1** My favourite sport is ______________________ *(Trampolinspringen)*. **2** It looks ___________ *(einfach, schlicht)*, but it isn't. **3** Have you _______ *(jemals)* tried it?

Anne **4** Yes, I've tried it _______ *(einmal)* or _________ *(zweimal)*. I thought it was really difficult.

Harry And what's your favourite sport?

Anne **5** Oh, I like ball games like basketball, volleyball _____ *(usw.)*. They're great fun!

Lerntipp

Du verstehst viel mehr englische Wörter als du gelernt hast!

Wenn du z.B. einen Satz liest wie 'My favourite sport is trampolining', dann kommst du sofort auf die Bedeutung von 'trampolining', auch wenn du das Wort noch nicht gelernt hast. Dabei hilft dir natürlich die **Ähnlichkeit** des Wortes mit dem Wort 'Trampolin'. Aber vor allem hilft dir der **Zusammenhang**: In diesem Satz ist ja die Rede von Sport – also kannst du ziemlich sicher sein, dass es sich bei 'trampolining' wirklich um 'Trampolinspringen' handelt und nicht etwas völlig anderes gemeint ist.

So kannst du mit unbekannten Wörtern im Text umgehen:

1. Prüfe, ob das Wort **Ähnlichkeiten** mit einem deutschen Wort hat.
2. Studiere den **Zusammenhang**.
3. Ziehe deine Schlüsse!

13 Two parts

Match the two parts of each sentence. Draw lines.
There's one new word in this exercise. What is it? Do you understand it?

1 Alex has never been to London,	**a)** but I haven't started maths yet.
2 I tried banana juice once,	**b)** but I saw a fox once.
3 I've just finished my English homework,	**c)** but she hasn't answered yet.
4 I've never seen a badger,	**d)** but I haven't asked him yet.
5 Sandra has eaten potatoes a lot of times,	**e)** but he'd really like to go.
6 Luke sent a message to Carina,	**f)** but he can't remember much.
7 I'd really like to go out with Liam,	**g)** but I didn't like it.
8 Carlo has been to Germany before,	**h)** but she has never tried potato salad.

The new word is ___________. *I think it's* ___________ *in German.*

14 New words ▸ pp. 74–75

Find the English words for the German words in brackets and fill in the gaps.

Dad **1** Come on, Ken. Let's start tidying your ____________ *(Schrank)*. It's so full! What's this?

Ken **2** Oh, that. That's Leyla, my old ______ *(Spielzeug-)* elephant. Don't throw her away, please.

3 I'll __________ *(malen, streichen)* her and she'll look fine again.

Dad Well – OK. **4** And what's this __________ *(Stück, Teil)* of __________ *(Papier)*?

Ken Let me see. **5** Ah, yes, we __________ *(befestigten)* it to the ________ *(Tor)* for my birthday party last year. Do you remember? Let's keep it, please!

Dad Really? OK. But what's this? **6** A ____________ *(zerbrochene, kaputte)* ____________ *(Kassette)*?

Ken That must be yours, Dad. It isn't mine!

Dad OK. **7** That's for the ____________ *(Abfall, Müll)* then. But what about all the other things in here?

Ken I know! **8** Let's have a garage ________ *(Verkauf, Ausverkauf)*. **9** Maybe some people will ______ *(zahlen)* a little for the old things.

Dad Good idea, Ken. **10** I'm going to write some __________ *(Etiketten, Schildchen)*.

Ken Great. **11** I'll get us a __________ *(Getränk)*. **12** Is ____________ *(Zitronenlimonade)* OK?

Dad Sure.

15 Partner words

Find the 10 partners.

piece, ~~buy~~, lemonade, cupboard, meal, gate, pen, label, price, toy, drink, fence, game, orange juice, paper, part, ~~pay~~, money, sign, wardrobe

buy – pay ____________

____________ ____________ ____________

____________ ____________ ____________ ____________

____________ ____________ ____________ ____________

____________ ____________ ____________ ____________

____________ ____________ ____________ ____________

16 The right words

Complete the sentences with a word from each side.

1 We'll be in the car for two hours. Let's take two bottles of cola.

2 Would you like a ________________ of chocolate ________________? Anton made it yesterday.

3 My grandma always has a nice, hot ________________ of ________________ and some biscuits in the afternoon.

4 Can you bring a ________________ of ________________ and some milk from the supermarket, please? We haven't got enough for breakfast tomorrow.

5 It's hot outside. Would you like a ________________ of ________________? I made it this morning.

6 Are you hungry? We can open a ________________ of ________________ if you like.

17 The right verb

Complete the sentences. Choose the right verb and put it in the right form.

be
paint
sell
save
~~steal~~

A week ago, somebody stole (1) our garden gate! My parents ________________ (2) very angry. But then they ________________ (3) an interesting company on the internet. They ________________ (4) everything and they are not expensive. My parents ________________ (5) a lot of things there – and they ________________ (6) a lot of money! On Saturday the postman ________________ (7) a big box with all the things. At the weekend, my father and my sister ________________ (8) the new gate to the fence and my mother and I ________________ (9) the garden shed blue. Everything is looking fine again now.

buy
find
deliver
fix

18 How often?

Make sentences. Say how often something has happened.

1 to · I've been · America · 1x:

I've been to America once.

2 trampolining · has tried · sister · My · 2x:

3 has seen · My · a cat · in · mum · our garden · 3x:

4 tennis · I've played · 1x or 2x:

5 caravan holiday · a · We've had · about · 10x:

6 in-line skating · I've done · xxxxxxxxxxxx (etc):

19 Right or wrong?

Say if these statements are right or wrong.

	Right	Wrong
1 In a shop you can usually find the price of clothes on a special label.	✔	☐
2 Children love to eat rubbish for breakfast.	☐	☐
3 If your pet is ill, you take it to a vet.	☐	☐
4 Yesterday is the past, and tomorrow is the present.	☐	☐
5 Most people keep their butter in a purse in the kitchen.	☐	☐
6 You must be careful with broken glass because it can hurt you.	☐	☐

20 Word groups

Put the German words on the right into English and find the right place for them in the list.

food	jobs	places of work
bean		

21 Word snake

Read the German meanings in the box below and complete the word snake.

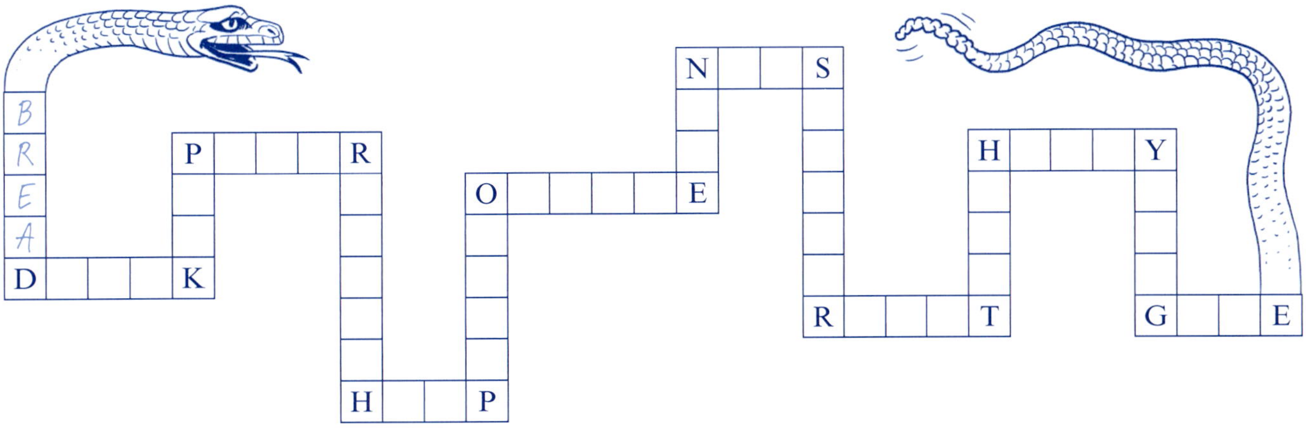

Abfall, Müll • ~~Brot~~ • Büro • finanziell unterstützen • Getränk • halten, behalten • hart, zäh • Hilfe • Honig • jung • Kartoffel • Neuigkeiten, Nachrichten • Papier • Roboter • Tor • verdienen

22 Numbers and letters

Each number is a letter.
Complete the sentences and find the secret sentence.

1 Jessica's dad works in a _ a _ _ _ _ _ .
20 6 4 22 1 7 21

2 Simon _ _ _ _ _ _ _ _ newspapers on Sunday morning.
17 9 12 16 15 9 7 3

3 In the future _ _ _ _ _ _ _ _ _ and _ _ _ _ _ _ will do all our work for us.
4 1 5 19 8 22 9 7 3 — 7 1 13 1 22 3

4 Oh no! Rusty has just eaten all our _ _ _ d _ _ _ _ _ _ !
3 6 14 17 11 16 4 2 9 3

5 Lynn sold her tennis _ _ _ _ _ t in a _ _ _ _ _ _ sale last weekend.
7 6 4 18 9 22 — 10 6 7 6 10 9

The secret sentence:

11 9 14 17 21 — 2 6 3 — 14 9 15 9 7 — 17 1 14 9 — 22 7 6 5 19 1 12 16 14 16 14 10

13 8 22 — 3 2 9 — 2 6 3 — 13 9 9 14 — 16 14 — 6 — 10 1 - 18 6 7 22 — 7 6 4 9 .

23 Missing words

Complete the sentences with the missing word (???), the opposite of the word (><) or a synonym for the word (>>).

1 On weekdays, we eat cornflakes with ________ (???) for breakfast. **2** But on Sundays we usually have a ______ (>< small) meal in the morning. **3** My dad ___________ (>< closes) a ______ (???) of beans and my mum makes a salad. **4** I make a lot of tea for us ________________ (>> kids) and _____________ (???) for my parents. **5** Then we _______________ (>< stand up) and enjoy the meal. **6** I like jam, but I really ________ (>> don't like) orange _____________________ (???). **7** And I love bread with a lot of _____________ (???) and honey. Hmmm! **8** I think it's _____________ (>< worse) than cake or chocolate. Sunday breakfasts are great! **9** And after the meal we all go for a ________ (>> journey) to the seaside or to the country. It's a lot of fun!

Now look at the answers to this exercise on p. 11 in the answer key[1]. *How many of your answers are right?*

12 or 11: Fantastic! **10–8:** Very good! **7–6:** Good!

5–3: You must practise more. **2 or 1:** Talk to your teacher.

MY LEARNER LOG

Mein Lerntagebuch. Hier notierst du deine Erfahrungen mit dem Wörterlernen.

♥ Meine drei englischen Lieblingswörter aus dieser Unit sind:

____

Wenn ich über die Zukunft sprechen will, kann ich diese neuen englischen Wörter sehr gut gebrauchen:

____

Besonders gern spreche ich mit den Wörtern aus dieser Unit darüber,

wie Erwachsene und Kinder Geld verdienen können: ☐

wie die Zukunft (allgemein, für mich oder für andere) aussehen wird: ☐

was ich schon einmal gemacht habe: ☐

Ich finde es sehr wichtig / recht wichtig / eher unwichtig, dass ich jetzt auf Englisch

Verabredungen treffen kann:	sehr wichtig ☐	recht wichtig ☐	eher unwichtig ☐
auf eine Nachricht reagieren kann:	sehr wichtig ☐	recht wichtig ☐	eher unwichtig ☐
anderen meine Hilfe anbieten kann:	sehr wichtig ☐	recht wichtig ☐	eher unwichtig ☐

[1] **answer key** [ki:] Lösungsschlüssel

1 New words ▸ p. 78

Find the English words for the German words in brackets and fill in the gaps.

Joe Hi. We're Jill and Joe. **1** We're thirteen-year-old __________________ *(Teenager)* and we're __________ *(Zwillinge)* – but we're very different.

Jill **2** We don't like the same colours or the same games, and we never watch TV together because we don't like the same ______________________ *(Sendungen)*.

Joe **3** I like ______________________ *(Seifenopern)*. **4** I like to talk to my friends about what will happen to the ____________________ *(Figuren, Charakteren)*. It's fun.

Jill **5** And I like ________________ *(Komödien)*. **6** My favourite ___________ *(Serie)* is about a family. **7** They've got a __________ *(Geist)* in the house, but they don't know it. It's so funny.

Joe **8** But we both hate ________________ *(Zeichentrickfilme)*, so that's easy.

Jill **9** When ____________ *(Gäste)* come to our house and they _________ *(treffen)* us for the first time, they think it's very strange that __________ *(Zwillinge)* can be so different.

Joe **10** Next week we're going to watch a ___________________________________ *(Wissenschafts-sendung)* on TV together. **11** They ____________ *(testeten)* __________ *(Zwillinge)* to find out if they all like the same things. That will be interesting!

2 Puzzle 'TV etc'

Read the definitions and write the eight words. What's the mystery word?

c

1 A "person" that doesn't really exist: _ _ _ _ t

2 A trip to see wild animals in Africa: _ _ _ _ _ _

3 A funny programme without real people: _ _ _ _ _ _ _ n

4 A series about the lives and problems of a group of people: _ _ _ _ _ _ _ _ _

5 A funny programme or film: _ _ _ _ _ _

6 Two children from the same family with the same birthday: _ _ _ _ _

7 People that come to your house because you asked them to come: _ _ _ _ t _

8 A group of programmes with the same characters etc: _ _ _ _ _ s

➜ *An animal can also be a* ________________ *in a book or a film.*

3 New words ▸ p. 79

Find the English words for the German words in brackets and fill in the gaps.

1 Last week my parents ______________ *(luden ein)* a man to our house. **2** He told us about a fantastic way to earn a lot of money: All members of a family ______________ *(werden)* ______________ *(Schauspieler/innen)* in a ______________________ *(Dokumentarfilm)*. **3** Well, it's not a real ______________________ *(Dokumentarfilm)*, it's more like a show. **4** Our ______________ *(Besucher)* explained that people who watch the show then ______________ *(entscheiden)* if you go on to the next ___________ *(Runde)* or not. **5** He said that families before us ______________ *(wurden)* very _______ *(reich)*. But my mum only laughed at him. **6** 'We're TV ________________ *(Dinosaurier)*,' she said. 'We're not interested in these new programmes.' And then he left. What a pity!

4 Two parts

For each word find its other part on the TVs – but be careful: the letters are jumbled.

1 car*toon*
2 ____________acter
3 come____________
4 din____________
5 ____________tary

6 milli____________
7 pro____________
8 ____________ence
9 ____________ger
10 visi____________

5 Missing words in jumbled sentences

Make the sentences. Careful: You must also add some missing (little) words.

My family really needs four TVs, because:

1 sports programmes • watches • always • father

My father always watches the sport programmes.

2 watches • news • mother • often ______________________________

3 that likes • only • brother • the • documentaries • family member

____

4 watch • day • favourite • I • soap opera • every • must

____

5 doesn't • little • watch • sister • yet • TV • only

____

6 New words ▸ pp. 80–81

Find the English words for the German words in brackets and fill in the gaps.

1 I had a strange ____________ *(Traum)* last night. I dreamed I was getting a prize. **2** I didn't ________________________ *(verstand nicht)* what the prize was for. **3** I was wearing a white jacket and a long black __________ *(Rock)*. **4** I was ____________ing *(erwartete)* flowers or some sweets, but then a man came and gave me a funny thing. **5** It looked like a ____ *(Musikinstrument)*. I blew into it and it made a terrible sound. The noise woke me up[1] – it was my mobile phone!

7 That can't be right!

Two (!) words are in the wrong place in each sentence. Cross them out and write the correct words.

1 Ken and Joe went to Hollywood to become ~~visitors~~ actors. In the summer they had lots of ~~actors~~ visitors from England.

2 Sam wore a black jacket and a white skirt. Anne wore a white jacket and a long black shirt with black shoes.

3 Louisa became a member of the school dream club because it was her drama to act in a film.

4 Tom showed his parents an instrument. 'Can I have this beautiful musical advertisement for my birthday, please?'

8 "ex"-words

Find the words. They all start with "ex".

1 Do … 13 for homework.

2 The film is really good. It's so …!

3 I don't understand this. Can you … it, please?

4 I haven't got enough money, it's too … .

5 I haven't got my umbrella. I didn't … the rain.

6 The project is going to be a lot of … work.

[1] **woke me up** [wəʊk] weckte mich

9 New words ▸ p. 82

Find the English words for the German words in brackets and fill in the gaps.

1 The fire alarm started ____ *(als, während)* Nick was looking at some sports clothes in the ____________ *(Mitte)* of the shopping centre. **2** He was ____________ *(innen, drinnen)* the shop, so he ____________ *(drehte)* back. **3** He knew he ____________ *(musste)* ____________ *(gehen zu, kommen zu)* the __________ *(Haupt-)* entrance. **4** He just ______________ *(folgte)* the other people. Suddenly everyone started running. 'How silly,' Nick thought – and then he fell. **5** He got up, and he ____________ *(beinahe)* fell again. **6** He felt like he was in a __________ *(Labyrinth)* and the people around him were the ____________ *(Hecken)*. Suddenly the shopping centre was empty. Where were all the people? **7** 'I don't want to ____________ *(mich verlaufen)*,' Nick thought. **8** 'At the next ____________ *(Abzweigung)*, I'll go right.' **9** But he came to a ______________ *(Sackgasse)*.
10 'I ______________ *(wahrscheinlich)* ____________ *(verpasste)* something,' he thought.
11 He took a very small path ______________ *(zwischen)* two shops – and then he was in his bed.
"Did you have a bad dream? You were shouting," his brother said.

10 Odd word out

Which word does not fit? Cross it out.

1 inside – middle – between – above – on
2 as – when – then – main – after
3 tree – flower – dream – hedge – bush
4 visit – invite – ghost – visitor – guest
5 millionaire – boy – teenager – girl – child
6 skirt – shirt – coat – maze – dress

11 Where's the ball?

Look at the pictures and say where the ball is in each picture.

1 It's ______________ the trees.
2 It's ______________ the tree.
3 It's ____ the chair.
4 It's ____________ the chair.
5 It's ____________________ the box.
6 It's probably ____________ the box.

12 The right word

Put each word in the right sentence, a) or b).

1a)

1b)

1 clean • lost
a) I always get ______________ in London.
b) I just can't get my dog ______________ today.

2 almost • always
a) Let's hurry. It's ______________ seven o'clock!
b) Not again! You're ______________ late for the film.

3 before • between
a) My favourite soap starts at 6, so I want to be home ______________ 5 and 6.
b) Mum, can I do one more game ______________ bed?

4 earn • turn
a) This is a dead end. Let's ______________ back.
b) I've got a new job. I have to ______________ some money for the holiday.

5 probably • really
a) I don't like the film. It's ______________ boring.
b) Where's Liz? – She's ______________ waiting for us outside.

6 lost • missed
a) The holiday was nice, but I ______________ my dog so much.
b) The holiday was nice, but I ______________ my purse.

7 as • if
a) Marc rang me on my mobile ______________ I was watching the film.
b) Don't use your mobile ______________ you watch a film in the cinema.

Lerntipp

Manche Wörter können je nach Zusammenhang mehrere Dinge bedeuten, z.B. das Verb *get*.
get ist eines der am häufigsten benutzten Wörter in der englischen Sprache.
Es hat viele verschiedene Bedeutungen – du kennst auch schon einige!

Am besten merkst du dir die verschiedenen Bedeutungen, wenn du dir beim Lernen ein Beispiel dazuschreibst:

get = bekommen, werden ▸ *get older*
get = holen ▸ *get the milk*

Aber manchmal steht ein Teil des Zusammenhangs auch schon fest, das macht das Lernen leichter.
Erinnerst du dich an die Bedeutung dieser Beispiele: *get clean, get home, get lost, get ready*?
Wenn nicht, schlag in deinem Buch auf S.160 nach und lies die Einträge zwischen *German* und *ghost*.

13 New words ▸ p. 83

Find the English words for the German words in brackets and fill in the gaps.

Mona Mum, Dad! We're back! Hi Mum, our garage sale was fantastic! First it was a bit slow, but ten minutes ago a man came and bought almost everything! **1** He bought the teddy bear with the missing ________ *(Ohren)*! **2** He bought Eva's picture of the woman whose ___________ *(Mund)* is above her _________*(Nase)*! It was great. This means we can now buy the present for your birth… Well. Where's dad, Mum? He'll be so happy for us!

Mum Oh, he went out. **3** Can you _______________ *(beschreiben)* the man, Mona?

Mona **4** Well, he was _______ *(groß)*. **5** I didn't see the colour of his ________ *(Augen)* because he was wearing sunglasses[1]. **6** He was probably wearing blue __________ *(Jeans)* and a black jacket, but I'm not sure. **7** I think he had a long ________ *(Gesicht)* like dad and his hair … well, it looked a bit like dad's hair … Oh, hi Dad! Where have you been?

Mum I think I know the answer.

14 Funny Face

a) *Look at the picture and complete the sentences with the right words.*

1 This Funny Face has got a very long ________ (almost like an elephant's _________).

2 It has got two ________ that look like little spiders.

3 It has got one big ______ on top of its head.

4 There's a ___________ in the middle of its face and another ___________ above it.

5 Funny Face's ________ looks a bit like the ________ of a horse.

6 Funny Face has got long spaghetti _______ on one side of its head.

b) *Draw your own Funny Face and describe it to your partner. Your partner has to draw it.*

[1] **sunglasses** ['sʌnglɑːsɪz] eine Sonnenbrille

15 New words ▸ pp. 86–89

Find the English words for the German words in brackets and fill in the gaps.

Liam **1** I'm a bit ______________ *(nervös)*. **2** My older sister has asked me to ____________ *(aufnehmen)* a programme for her. **3** It's on the science ______________ *(Kanal, Programm)*. **4** It's an old programme about the ______________ *(Verkehrs-)* situation in London twenty years ago. Mia needs it for a project. **5** I want to do her a ____________ *(Gefallen)* and I want to do it _______ *(gut)*. Let's see. **6** She said I ____________ *(sollte)* take the ________ *(Band)* that's in the blue box on the shelf. Is this it? **7** Well, it's really blue and green, but the _______ *(Rest)* of the video boxes here are all black.

(Later …)

Mia You stupid little idot! I said the blue box, not the blue-green box. Do you know what you've done? **8** You've _________________ *(aufgenommen)* over a ________ *(Band)* that was __________ *(wert)* a lot of money!

Liam **9** But it's not my _________ *(Fehler, Schuld)*! There was no other blue box on the shelf. **10** You're so _________ *(gemein)*!

Mia But … Sorry, Liam. You're right. When I remembered that the blue box was in the cupboard, not on the shelf, I tried to phone you. **11** I _____________ *(wählte)* your number but I didn't get through. I'm really sorry, OK?

Liam OK. I'm sorry, too.

16 Situations

What you can say in these situations? Use one of these words in each answer:
fault · have to · pity · should

1 Wie reagierst du, wenn jemand sagt, er/sie könne nicht zu deiner Geburtstagsfeier kommen?

That's ____

2 Wie verteidigst du dich, wenn jemand dir vorwirft, du seist zu spät gekommen?

Yes, but ____

3 Wie empfiehlst du jemandem, das gelbe T-Shirt (und nicht das grüne) zu kaufen?

Well, I think ____

4 Wie erklärst du jemandem, dass die Aufgabe einfach zu lösen ist, wenn man zuerst die Antworten liest?

That's easy. Look. You just ______________________________ first.

17 Missing letters

The missing letters are the same in each pair of words. Put them in.
(If you need help: The first word of each pair is in the box below – jumbled and in German.)

1 di_a_l – t_a_ll
2 ta_e – soa_
3 fau_t – shou_d
4 rec__d – w__th
5 tra__ic – o__ice
6 ca__van – pa__graph
7 __come – __tween
8 fa___r – ner___s
9 tun___ – chan___
10 can___ – mid___

nahmeufne | refleh | flegalne | zeerk | deanbivod | lunten | krehver | ~~lewähn~~ | gewannwoh | drewen

18 That's wrong! What's right?

There are two mistakes in each sentence. Cross them out and write the correct words.

1 Carl is very nervous because ~~yesterday~~ is her first day as a policeman in England.

today ______ ______

2 Their has just been an accident and someone dialled 911, the telephone letter for the police in England.

______ ______

3 Now Carl have to drive there quickly threw a lot of traffic.

______ ______

4 He must record that he has to drives on the left side of the road!

______ ______

5 The accident wasn't bad but both driver say it was the other driver's favour.

______ ______

6 Carl takes no photos becourse that's part of his job when there's an accident.

______ ______

19 Adjective puzzle

Find the eight adjectives in the word puzzle on the right.

______ ______
______ ______
______ ______
______ ______

EARMEANNERVOUSFAVOUR
TALLDIALFAULTRICHMOUTH
EYEBROKENMISSSKIRTNOSE
SIMPLEFACEFAIRTESTCLEAN

20 Odd word out

Read the words aloud[1] and decide which pronunciation (!) does not fit the group. Cross it out.

1 head – bed – ~~pet~~ – said

2 eye – lie – why – say

3 wear – year – hair – there

4 knows – nose – lose – close

5 here – where – ear – deer

6 case – face – maze – space

21 Silly sentence

Match the words on the right to the phonetic symbols and find the mystery (silly) sentence.

____

ʃi ʃʊd 'prɒbəbli du mi ə

____

'feɪvə ənd ɪn'vaɪt ə gest

______________________________ .

ˌɪn'saɪd 'auə meɪz

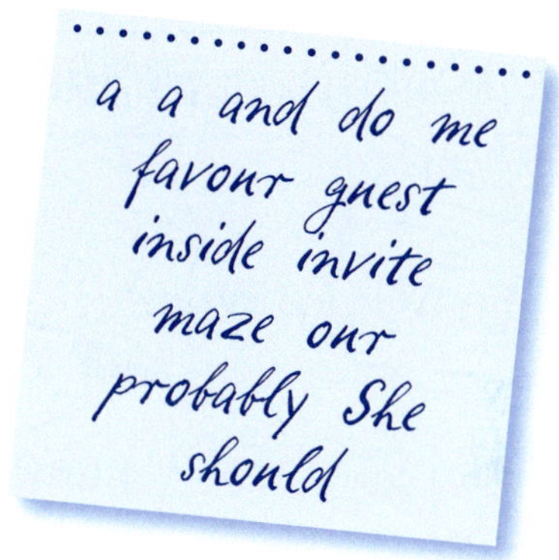

22 Word families

a) *Complete the table.*

	Verb	Noun		Verb	Noun (Person)
1	drink	drink	5		actor
2	sell		6	drive	
3		test	7		teacher
4	turn		8	visit	

b) *Complete the sentences with a word from the table above.*

1 It's hot today. Would you like a drink?

2 If you go left at the ____________, you'll see the station in front of you.

3 I'd like to move to Hollywood and become a famous ____________ .

4 If you don't use your in-line skates, you should try to ____________ them.

5 When I was in hospital, I had a lot of ____________ .

6 Let's go outside. I want to ____________ my new model plane.

[1] **read aloud** [ə'laʊd] laut lesen

23 Word friends

Each verb (1–4) goes with only two of the words/phrases below. Circle the right two.

24 Network

Make a word network for 'Describing people'. You can use some of the new words below, too.

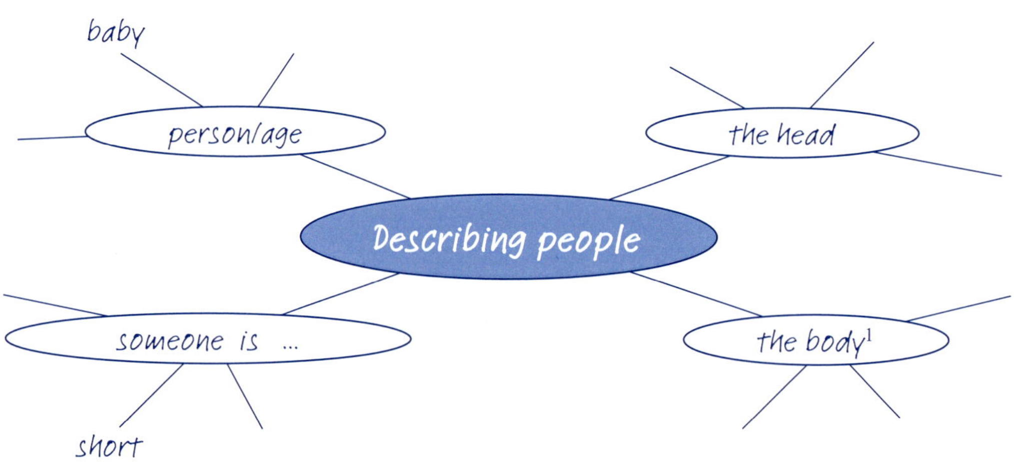

Some useful extra words:
bald [bɔːld] glatzköpfig; **beard** [bɪəd] Bart; **brace** [breɪs] Zahnspange; **curly hair** ['kɜːli] Locken, lockige Haare; **freckles** ['freklz] Sommersprossen; **glasses** ['glaːsɪz] Brille; **thin** [θɪn] dünn

[1] **body** ['bɒdi] Körper

25 Missing words

Complete the sentences with the missing word (???), the opposite of the word (><) or a synonym for the word (>>).

1 In the holidays, Dan and Jake went on a little ________ (>> journey). Their plan was to test the maze at Hampton Court. **2** "The maze can't be very ___________ (>> hard). **3** My sister did it in one hour last month," Dan said ____ (>> when) they were waiting in the queue at the _________________ (???). **4** They bought their tickets and went ____________ (>< outside). "OK," Dan said. **5** Let's ________ (>< lose) the _____________ (>> centre) then." **6** But soon they got _______ (???). After about one hour, Dan turned to talk to Jake – and fell. **7** He only hurt his arm a _____ (>< lot). **8** "I'm ________ (>> happy) you're OK," Jake said. "Let's go now." **9** It wasn't ________ (>< hard) but then they got out. **10** "I think we did that _______ (>< badly)," Dan said. "We're as good as my sister." **11** "But your sister was ____________ (>> quicker), wasn't she?" Jake said. **12** "Yes – but I'm sure a month ago the _____________ (???) weren't as high as they were today."

Now look at the answers to this exercise on p. 13 in the answer key[1]. How many of your answers are right?

14 or 13: Fantastic! **12–10:** Very good! **9–7**: Good!
6–3: You must practise more. **2 or 1:** Talk to your teacher.

MY LEARNER LOG

Mein Lerntagebuch. Hier notierst du deine Erfahrungen mit dem Wörterlernen.

♥ Meine drei englischen Lieblingswörter aus dieser Unit sind:

____

So gut kann ich jetzt auf Englisch …

(1) Menschen beschreiben: Ich gebe mir die Schulnote ____.
Beispiel *(Beschreibe ein Kind aus deiner Klasse.)*:

____

2) über das Fernsehangebot sprechen: Ich gebe mir die Schulnote ____.
Beispiel *(Beschreibe deine Lieblingssendung.)*:

____

3) mit Präpositionen angeben, wo sich etwas befindet: Ich gebe mir die Schulnote ____.
Beispiel *(Gib an, wo sich dein Englischbuch gerade befindet.)*:

____

[1] **answer key** [kiː] Lösungsschlüssel

1 New words ▸ p. 94

Find the English words for the German words in brackets and fill in the gaps.

Dylan **1** What __________ *(Zustand)* are we in, Joe?

Johannes What do you mean? We're very tired! We've been in this car for six hours.

Dylan No, I mean: **2** What __________ *(Staat)* are we driving through at the moment?

Johannes Oh, I don't know. **3** ________ *(Riesige)* _____________ *(goldene)* _______________ *(Wüsten)*, no trees, no lakes, no people.

Dylan It's probably Arizona. **4** Did you know that Hollywood made some famous westerns here – cowboy _____________ *(Filme; AE)*, you know?

Johannes I know what westerns are, but Hollywood? That's in California.

Dylan Yes, but they sometimes came over here to the old western towns. You can visit them. It's great.

Johannes No, thank you. **5** I just want to arrive at the ____________ *(Ferienort)*. **6** I want to see the famous ____________________ *(Wasserfälle)* and ____________ *(Bergkämme, Grate)* in the ________________ *(National-)* park. **7** And I want to _____ *(Ski fahren)*, like I do at home in Bavaria!

Dylan Yes, I know. Well, maybe we can visit a western town on the way back to Texas.

2 What do you mean?

Read the dialogues and put in the missing word.

1 We went to a, er, a 'skiing village'.

– Skiing village? What do you mean?

I mean a place with lots of hotels where people go for a skiing holiday.

– Oh, you mean a _____________!

2 We walked along the, er, 'mountain line'.

– Mountain line? What do you mean?

I mean a small part of the mountain at the top that you can walk on.

– Oh, you mean a ___________!

3 We drove through, er, 'dead country' for a time.

– Dead country? What do you mean?

I mean a place where you can't see people, trees or animals, because it's usually much too hot there.

– Oh, you mean a _____________!

4 It was great. We went, eh, 'riding on the sea'.

– Riding on the sea? What do you mean?

I mean a sport where you stand on a big piece of plastic on the water.

– Oh, you mean _______________!

3 New words ▸ p. 95

Find the English words for the German words in brackets and fill in the gaps.

Maisie We've just been to San Francisco. It's the best place in America! **1** Have you ever been up a ________ *(steilen)* ______ *(Hügel)* in a ______________ *(Kabelstraßenbahn)* and then enjoyed the great view from the top across the city __________ *(unten, unterhalb)*?

Scarlet No, I haven't. We're just back from Texas. **2** I swam in warm ___Stream___ *(Golfstrom)* water almost every day.

Maisie **3** Well, we didn't go swimming, but we visited an exciting prison museum on an __________ *(Insel)* in the __________ *(Meer, Ozean)*.

Scarlet Do you mean Alcatraz? **4** It isn't really in the __________ *(Meer, Ozean)*. **5** Well, we travelled ____________ *(endlose)* ______________ *(Hauptverkehrsstraßen)* all across the desert ________ *(Land, Boden)* of the south. It was fantastic.

Maisie Yes, well, we often went shopping. **6** My parents bought some expensive ________ *(Wein)* from Napa __________ *(Tal)*. And I bought a great pair of very high pink shoes.

Scarlet Funny. I bought a pair of shoes, too. Mine are black and blue and very good for walking.

4 Groups of words

Take the words from the box and make four groups of words that belong together.

~~country~~ • highway • hill • lake • ~~land~~ • mountain • ocean • ridge • road • sea • state • street

1	2	3	4
country			
land			

Lerntipp

Wörter, die du zu sinnvollen Gruppen zusammenfügst, behältst du besser!

Manchmal passt ein Wort in mehrere Gruppen. Wenn du mit Vokabelkarten lernst, füge sie immer wieder zu neuen Gruppen zusammen.

5 New words ▸ p.96

Find the English words for the German words in brackets and fill in the gaps.

Hi Angie,

Today our English teacher told us about American English. **1** Now I know why you sometimes use funny words and why you usually make ____________ *(viele)* 'mistakes' in the ________________ *(Rechtschreibung)* of words! **2** I also know that I'll need ______ *(Benzin; AE)* – not ____________ *(Benzin; BE)* – for my __________ *(Lastwagen; AE)* – not _________ *(Lastwagen; BE)* – when I go to America, ha, ha. **3** We all knew about _______________________ *(Pommes frites; AE)* of course, because all the big hamburger restaurants use the word. **4** And in these times of e-mail, etc I don't have to think long before I know what your verb '_________' *(schicken, aufgeben; AE)* means. **5** Well, let's hope that I can see America with my own eyes in the next summer holidays – sorry, _________________ *(Urlaub, Ferien; AE)*!

Love, Giulia

6 British and American English

Look at this advertisement for American tourists. The English hotel tried to use American English, but they made some mistakes.

Come and spend your vacation at the
King's Hotel in Brighton, England!

We're not far from the main road to the airport, but don't worry: you won't hear the trucks.
We're also not far from the center of Brighton – and we're neighbours to the best little restaurant in town. (You won't get chips there!)
In the evening, you can watch American movies or some of the famous British TV programmes in our huge living-room for guests.
We're easy to find: The color of our house is pink – and we're right behind the petrol station.

a) *Find the five wrong (British) words/spellings and put them into American English.*

main road → highway, ____________________

____

b) *And what's right? Find the five right American English words/spellings.*

vacation, ____________________

____

7 New words ▸ p. 98

Find the English words for the German words in brackets and fill in the gaps.

In Munich …

Speaker OK, fans: The game is going to start soon. Don't forget: You can listen to our report on the radio or – this is new – watch it on the internet. **1** Here are the German ____________ *(Spielerinnen)*. It won't be easy for them today. **2** And now let's ____________ *(willkommen heißen)* our guests: The basketball team from … Miami, Florida!

3 ____________ *(inzwischen)* **in Miami, Florida …**

Loreen **4** That ____________ *(hört sich … an)* fantastic, ______ *(Mama; AE)*, doesn't it? I'm so happy my big sister went to Munich with the team.

Grandad **5** Now, what's her ____________ *(Stellung, Lage)* again?

Loreen **6** She's a ____________ *(Fängerin)*, grandad.

Mom … perhaps not today. **7** Look, I've just found this bag with all her ____________ *(Ausrüstung)* in her room!

Loreen Oh no!

8 English words in Germany

There are many English words that we also use in German. Look at the list and add more words.

Here are some ideas: basketball, burger, comic, download, internet, jeans, party, smartphone, surfing, teenager, ticket, website, …

Clothes	Food, etc	Spare time	Sports	Technology, etc	Other words
cap	barbecue	camping	bowling	computer	jet lag

9 New words ▸ pp. 102–103

Find the English words for the German words in brackets and fill in the gaps.

Chuck Hi, I'm Chuck. **1** I'm the new ___________ *(Schlagmann)*.

Mason Who? Who sent you? We don't need you. **2** We need a _____________ *(Werfer)*.

Chuck But I'm really good. **3** I _____ *(treffe, schlage)* every ball!

Mason OK, let's see. Stand over there. Dan, can you throw a ball to Chuck here, please? …

(Bang!)

Chuck Oh, your bottle. **4** Your _____________ *(Werfer)* is terrible!

Mason That's what I mean. **5** We need a new _____________ *(Werfer)*, not a ____________ *(Schlagmann)*. Dan? **6** Come here and put the broken glass in the ______________ *(Müll, Abfall; AE)*. **7** At least[1] they can _____________ *(wieder aufbereiten, wieder verwerten)* it.

10 Puzzle 'People who do things'

Do the puzzle and find the mystery word.

1 A person who sings: _ _ _ _ _ _

2 A person who throws the ball in baseball: _ _ _ _ _ _ _

3 A person who plays chess/ball/…: _ _ _ _ _ _

4 A person who drives a car/bus/…: _ _ _ _ _ _

5 A person who hits the ball in baseball: _ _ _ _ _ _

6 A person who teaches people: _ _ _ _ _ _ _

7 A person who catches the ball in baseball: _ _ _ _ _ _ _

8 A person who plays football: _ _ _ _ _ _ _ _ _ _

9 A person who manages a company/shop/…: _ _ _ _ _ _ _

➜ *What does a ____________ do?? Oh, it's not a person, it's a thing!*

[1] **at least** [li:st] zumindest

11 New words ▸ pp. 104–106

Find the English words for the German words in brackets and fill in the gaps.

Mum **1** Let me give you a ________ (*Kuss*) before you go.

John No! I'm fine.

Mum **2** That's not very ________________ (*freundlich*).

John Oh, Mum, please. I just want to leave now.

Mum Are you sure you'll find it?

John **3** Well, I'll remember your ______________________ (*Erklärung*). **4** When I get off the bus, I'll go right to the _____________ (*Platz*).

5 The ________________ (*Gebäude*) is just behind the fountains[1] there.

Mum **6** _____________ (*Genau*)! **7** And don't let the children at the fountains ____________ (*bespritzen*) you.

John Mum!

Mum I know, I know. You're old enough. **8** Good ________ (*Viel Glück*) then.

12 Word families

a) *Complete the table.*

	Verb	Noun		Noun	Adjective
1	build	building	**5**		endless
2	explain		**6**	friend	
3		camping	**7**		funny
4	sound		**8**	luck	

b) *Complete each sentence with a word from the table above. Put the word in the right form.*

1 Is Hannah OK? Her voice ____________________ strange on the phone yesterday.

2 The problem with Henry is: His jokes are never ____________________.

3 I don't know why Mag is so angry. Have you got an ____________________?

4 I really like Adam. He's always polite and ____________________.

5 My mum's office is in the tall ____________________ over there.

[1] **fountain** ['faʊntən] Fontäne

13 Puzzle

Write the English words in the puzzle. Then take the marked letters and make the mystery word. Careful: They're not in the right order!

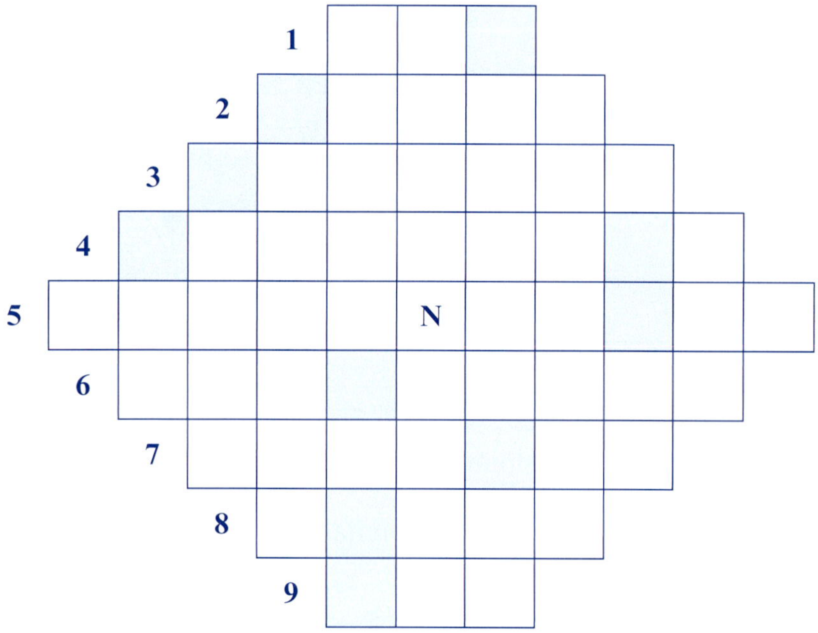

1 schlagen, treffen
2 genau
3 Müll, Abfall (BE)
4 Ausrüstung
5 Erklärung
6 inzwischen
7 Mission, Missionsstation
8 steil
9 Ski fahren

➜ *This is so boring. Can't we do something more*

										G

?

14 The fourth[1] word

Find the fourth word.
Tip: *The words are all on the right – but the letters and words are in the wrong order.*

1 road – highway town – city
2 mountain – (to) ski ocean – (to) __________
3 lorry – petrol truck – __________
4 batter – (to) hit catcher – (to) __________
5 up – down above – __________
6 legs – jeans head – __________
7 friendly – nice exact – __________
8 movie – film (to) mail – (to) __________

pac
gsa
~~icyt~~
hacct
miws
webol
creroct
stop

[1] **fourth** [fɔːθ] vierte/r/s

15 "re"-words

Find the words. They all start with "re".

1 My grandad always wants to … music from the radio.

2 I only had one New Year's …, but I didn't keep it.

3 Do you … your first day at school?

4 Do you know the … of the football game?

5 I'm sorry – can you please … your question?

6 Have you read Linda's … in the school magazine?

7 If you … glass, you can make new bottles from it.

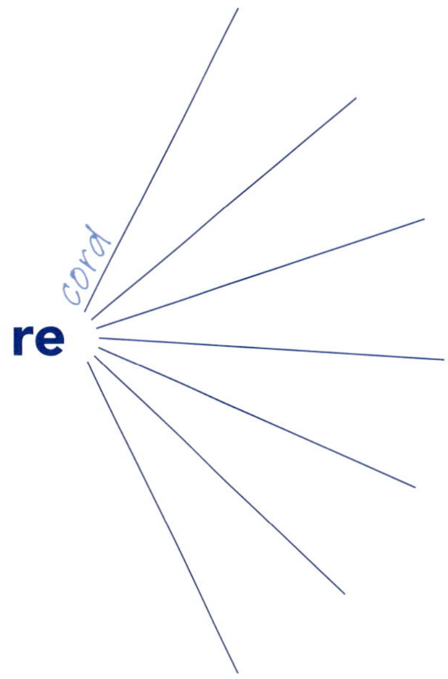

16 Three words

Complete each sentence with three words from the box. Careful! You don't need all the words.

batter • bowling • burgers • camping • catcher • french fries • friendly • hit • ~~island~~ • lorries • mean • nervous • pitcher • plotter • potatoes • resort • skyway • splash • steep • stop • surfing • turn • turning • valley

1 The holiday was fantastic! We went to our favourite island / ____________ / ____________.

2 You have to be more careful. You eat too many ____________ / ____________ / ____________.

3 We always go ____________ / ____________ / ____________ in our holiday.

4 My daughter likes baseball. She's a ____________ / ____________ / ____________ on the school team.

5 Do you know Joshua? He's a very ____________ / ____________ / ____________ boy.

6 Don't ____________ / ____________ / ____________ that elephant!

17 Missing words

Complete the sentences with the missing word (???), the opposite of the word (><), a synonym for the word (>>) or the British English word for an American English word (AE).

1 Hi Alicia, I'm having a horrible ______________ (AE: vacation). **2** We're on a very __________ (>< huge) island. **3** There's almost _______________ (>< everything) here: No cars, no kids, no fun – it's so ____________ (>< exciting)! **4** I can't go shopping, because there are no __________ (???). **5** I can't watch __________ (AE: movies), because there are no _______________ (???), no TVs and no computers! **6** So I _____ (>< stand) on the beach every ______ (>< night) and read books. **7** I've just read a __________________ (>> wonderful) book about a ________________ (>> very nice) man who lives on an island on his own before he meets another _______ (???). But he can't understand him. **8** He __________ (???) him the name 'Friday' and then they … **9** Oh, I'll ________ (>< borrow) you the book when I'm back home. **10** I'll also give you this letter when I'm back – because I can't ________ (AE: mail) it here! Love, Megan

Now look at the answers to this exercise on p. 15 in the answer key[1]*. How many of your answers are right?*

15 or 14: Fantastic! **13–11:** Very good! **10–7:** Good!

6–3: You must practise more. **2 or 1:** Talk to your teacher.

MY LEARNER LOG

Mein Lerntagebuch. Hier notierst du deine Erfahrungen mit dem Wörterlernen.

♥ Meine drei englischen Lieblingswörter aus dieser Unit sind:

____

Am Ende dieses *Wordmaster*-Heftes gebe ich mir folgende Englisch-Noten von 1 (= sehr gut) bis 5 (= mangelhaft):

(beim Sprechen) für meine Aussprache: ____

(beim Lesen oder Hören) für das Wiedererkennen von Wörtern: ____

(beim Sprechen oder Schreiben) für die Benutzung von Wörtern, die schon vorgekommen sind: ____

(beim Lesen oder Hören) für das Verstehen von Texten, auch wenn ich nicht alle Wörter kenne: ____

(beim Schreiben) für die richtige Schreibweise von Wörtern: ____

★ Im nächsten Schuljahr möchte ich vor allem besser ______________________ lernen.

[1] **answer key** [ki:] Lösungsschlüssel

1 A "cross*verb*" puzzle

Read the sentences below and put the missing verbs in the crossword. They have to be in the correct form!

Across ▸

1 Can you speak more slowly? I can't ★ you.
5 You can ★ lots of money in this job.
6 Come home soon. I ★ you so much!
8 Mum is ★ the bathroom walls blue.
10 Sh! I'm ★ the game on the radio.
11 When you start the machine, the wheel ★.
13 I only ★ £3 for a huge breakfast.
14 Dinosaurs ★ a long time ago.
17 School finishes at 4, so Lou will ★ at 4.30.
19 The princess will ★ queen in a few years.
21 Dad has just ★ our old car for £200.
23 I'm ★ my money for the summer holiday.
24 My grandma only ★ hens on her farm.

Down ▾

2 Can you ★ the boy who hurt you?
3 Mel ★ newspapers at the weekend.
4 After the accident dad quickly ★ 999.
7 Wow! Jay has just ★ me to his party!
9 I'm so happy for you – it ★ really fantastic!
12 Someone has ★ my purse!
14 My mum ★ a visitor today.
15 Red or green? I can't ★ !
16 Ruby ★ the sign to the door yesterday.
18 I ★ Lenny at the cinema last week.
20 I can't come. My brother ★ my bike.
22 You can't ★ a player. It's not fair.

2 Secret messages

These are secret messages. What do they mean?
(There's some help at the bottom of the page. Only look at it if you really don't know what to do!)

Tomorrow me with cinema the to go to like you would?

1 This message means:

____

____

Somelomebolodyly islis wailistingling forlor youlou atlat thele mainlain enlentrancelance oflof thele schoollool.

2 This message means:

____

____

Rehtegot ytrap yadhtrib eht ot og ew nac?

3 This message means:

____

____

Dpnf boe uffu uf bu uif hbsefo hbuf upojhiu.

4 This message means:

____

____

Help:
Message 1: Turn it around.
Message 2: Take some letters out.
Message 3: Back to front.
Message 4: -1 letter.

Unit 1

1 New words
1 lively, city
2 famous, sights, city centre
3 bells
4 palace, centre
5 interesting, bus tour
6 Tower
7 prison
8 exciting
9 by, river, River
10 bridges, famous, parliament
11 lively
12 fire-eaters, jugglers

2 Tips for London
1 famous
2 interesting
3 exciting
4 lively

3 Word ladder
2 bell
3 ball
4 hall
5 wall
6 walk

4 Make the words
2 exciting
3 famous
4 interesting
5 juggler
6 lively
7 palace
8 parliament
9 prison
10 river
11 sights
12 tower

5 Jumbled sentences
1 Can you show me the sights of London, please?
2 I'd like to take a tour of the old prison in London.
3 Let's take a boat on the lake in Hyde Park on Sunday.

6 New words
1 underground line, Street
2 Circle Line
3 Queen
4 Millennium Dome
5 central
6 south-east
7 tube
8 build, wood, clay
9 Bricks, stones

7 Puzzle 'In London'
1 dome
2 circle
3 bell
4 juggler
5 Bridge
6 Queen
7 stone
8 brick
9 tube
10 Thames

The mystery word: *millennium*

8 More questions and answers
1 Which – c)
2 How – d)
3 What – f)
4 Who – g)
5 Where – a)
6 When – e)
7 Whose – h)
8 Why – b)

9 Word partners
1 lively
2 exciting
3 palace
4 underground
5 street
6 by
7 clay
8 stones
9 east
10 bell
11 bridge
12 line

10 Odd word out
2 tour
3 circle
4 river
5 centre

11 New words
1 husband
2 son
3 cousin
4 daughter
5 wife
6 aunt

12 Families
2 wife
3 mother
4 mum
5 aunt
6 daughter
7 sister
8 cousin

13 Where are they?
1 south-east
2 south
3 north
4 north-east
5 east
6 west

14 New words
1 museum
2 tourists, popular with
3 Museum
4 waxworks, a lot of
5 If, queue, short
6 cheap
7 way

15 Definitions
1 cheap
2 popular
3 short
4 tourist
5 footballer
6 museum
The mystery word: *famous*

16 Sentences
Lösungsvorschlag:
2 go, quickest, way
3 see, famous, people
4 hear, famous, bell
5 visit, famous, Tower
6 eat, cheapest, food

17 New words
1 argument
2 hopeless
3 Don't worry
4 Looking forward to
5 ticket, pocket
6 don't worry
7 busy
8 Don't worry
9 chamber of horrors
10 world
11 Don't worry
12 look after
13 no
14 Don't worry

18 Pronunciation
a)
[ɑː] *after*, dance, half, part
[ɜː] circle, learn, shirt, work
[ɔː] daughter, door, form, walk
[iː] cheap, cheese, eat, street

b) The short queen of the east is the best aunt in the world.

19 New words
1 polite
2 more, than
3 cross, rule
4 missing, left

20 Word web
2 please
3 plane
4 path
5 prison
6 polite
7 public
8 palace
9 push
10 pocket
11 phone
12 plate

21 Definitions
2 A
3 E
4 C
5 F
6 D

22 New words
1 outside
2 rain
3 jokes
4 jokes, better
5 slogan, advertisement
6 as, as
7 worse
8 boring
9 worst

23 Missing words
(1) great
(2) much
(3) than
(4) very
(5) as
(6) as
(7) best
(8) worse
(9) than
(10) more
(11) than
(12) worst
(13) as
(14) as

24 New words
1 over there
2 look
3 are smiling
4 presenter
5 president
6 royal
7 king, princess
8 singer, over there
9 He's fed up
10 own
11 criminals
12 horrible, scenes, torture
13 never mind

25 People and things
a)
aunt, child, cousin, criminal, daughter, fire-eater, footballer, grandad, husband, juggler, kid, king, lady, parents, presenter, president, princess, queen, relative, singer, son, tourist, wife

b)
Verschiedene Antworten möglich.

26 New words
1 letters
2 models
3 model
4 pigs
5 show

27 The right word
2 letters
3 letters
4 show
5 stew
6 show

28 Network
Verschiedene Antworten möglich.

29 Word groups
Tourists They look at … bridges, museums, palaces, towers, waxworks
There are sights in the … north, east, south, west, centre

TV You can see … films, presenters, quiz shows, advertisements, singers
It's often … exciting, horrible, great, interesting, boring

30 Crossword puzzle
Across ▸ :
1 part
4 bridge
5 popular
7 rule
9 which
12 queue
15 parliament
17 show
19 short
20 model
21 build

Down ▾ :
1 pig
2 line
3 polite
6 argument
8 lively
9 way
10 hopeless
11 cheap
13 horrible
14 circle
16 busy
17 from
19 wood

31 The fourth word
2 worst
3 princess
4 cheap
5 aunt
6 west
7 prison
8 palace

32 Three words
1 *better* / cheaper / worse
2 awful / boring / horrible
3 build / cross / see
4 footballer / juggler / singer
5 exciting / interesting / lively
6 a lot of / more / no

Unit 2

1 New words
1 grandparents, in the country
2 farm
3 cows
4 horses, ponies
5 sheep, hens
6 animals, farm
7 cottages

2 What is it?
1 horse
2 pig
3 cow
4 cat
5 pony
6 sheep

3 That can't be right!
2 pigs ▸ relatives, relatives ▸ pigs
3 rabbits ▸ hutches, hutches ▸ rabbits
4 budgies ▸ daughters, daughters ▸ budgies

4 New words
1 lovely, stream
2 lie, ground, birds
3 air, flowers
4 swallows
5 everywhere, deer
6 young, deer, lovely

5 Funny animals
2 a + **5 b** = horse
3 a + **4 b** = pig
4 a + **1 b** = cow
5 a + **3 b** = sheep
6 a + **2 b** = hen

6 Right or wrong?
2 ✔
3 ✔
4 ✔
5 ✔
6 ✘
7 ✘
8 ✘
9 ✔
10 ✔

7 New words
1 yesterday, ill
2 Last, dream
3 washed, hair
4 Everyone
5 You were
6 someone, Stop
7 stopped
8 dream, diary
9 tomorrow
10 project

8 The right word
(2) was
(3) weren't
(4) is
(5) wasn't
(6) are
(7) aren't
(8) isn't

9 When?
1 yesterday
2 tomorrow
3 today
4 tomorrow
5 yesterday

10 New words
1 happened
2 past
3 sea, sun
4 village
5 forest
6 did

11 Missing verbs
(1) went
(2) thought
(3) got
(4) saw
(5) rode
(6) did
(7) drove
(8) said

12 New words
1 story
2 love
3 A long time ago, coast
4 badgers, wild
5 cool
6 felt
7 into, head
8 light
9 dark
10 head, guide
11 light
12 at the front
13 moment, noise
14 along, side
15 badger, badgers, guess

13 Word snail
cottage, farm, swallow, sun, badger, air, flower, forest, animal, stream, coast
Lösungswort: *grandparents*

14 Odd word out
1 air
2 start
3 sheep
4 ground
5 guess
6 badger

15 Crossword puzzle
Across ▸ :
1 thought
4 took
6 stopped
8 did
9 drove
13 lived
15 rode
16 saw
19 went
20 stayed

Down ▾ :
2 happened
3 posted
4 tidied
5 borrowed
6 said
7 made
10 closed
11 flew
12 felt
14 moved
17 was
18 lay

16 New words
1 conversation
2 interview
3 both
4 Are you afraid of
5 against
6 Do you … sleep
7 catch my bus

17 Opposites
1 hate
2 start
3 stand
4 yesterday
5 for
6 old
7 last
8 into
9 foot
10 rain

18 New words
1 paramedic
2 bored
3 carried, stretcher, ambulance
4 Suddenly, strange
5 rang, mobile phone, paramedics
6 shock, fell off, stretcher
7 landed, back
8 voice, nothing
9 Keep, calm
10 explained, lift, stretcher, off
11 sad
12 sad
13 mobile phone

19 The right word
1 **a)** *after*, **b)** for
2 **a)** against, **b)** again
3 **a)** voice, **b)** noise
4 **a)** bored, **b)** boring

20 Puzzle
1 worry
2 shock
3 stretcher
4 paramedic
5 lie
6 carry
7 hospital
8 accident
9 ill
10 hurt
The mystery word: *wheelchair*

21 One German word = Two English words
1 **a)** *side*, **b)** page
2 **a)** ago, **b)** before
3 **a)** wears, **b)** carry
4 **a)** quiet, **b)** still
5 **a)** bag, **b)** pocket
6 **a)** about, **b)** over

22 The simple past
a) **Across ▸ :**
bought, spoke, caught, wore, rang, thought, found, heard, drank, fell, told

Down ▾ :
took, won, ate, hurt

b) buy – bought, speak – spoke, catch – caught, wear – wore, ring – rang, think – thought, find – found, hear – heard, drink – drank, fall – fell, tell – told, take – took, eat – ate, hurt – hurt

c) *Verschiedene Antworten möglich.*

d) (2) caught
(3) rang
(4) sang
(5) kept
(6) slept

23 Missing letters
2 bird
3 cottage
4 grandparents
5 ground
6 guess
7 guide
8 head
9 light
10 strange
11 stretcher
12 through

24 Word groups
jobs: guide, officer, paramedic, policeman, postman, teacher
conversation: ask, explain, interview, say, talk, *tell*
animals: badger, cow, deer, horse, pig, *pony*, sheep
to feel …: *afraid*, angry, bored, happy, sad, tired

25 Three words
1 *lovely* / strange / wild
2 birds / horses / villages
3 best / first / last
4 air / coast / sea
5 A lot / Nothing / Something
6 against / past / through

Unit 3

1 New words
1 elephants
2 DVD
3 disc
4 screen
5 click on, print, find out

2 Little words
1 on
2 out
3 off
4 to
5 out
6 of, of

3 New words
1 history
2 searches for, websites
3 newspapers
4 up-to-date, news, internet
5 sends, e-mails
6 millions, messages
7 types, everything
8 results

4 Word groups
1 *e-mails*, internet, websites
2 books, magazines, newspapers
3 computers, discs, screens
4 French, history, maths
5 click on, print, send
6 phrases, sentences, words
7 deer, elephants, grizzly bears

5 That's wrong! What's right?
2 He clicked on 'Like'.
3 She sent me a postcard.
4 He rang me.
5 We felt excited.
6 I searched for basketball news.

6 Some words rhyme
caught – thought, found – pound, news – shoes, run – won, screen – mean, sent – meant

7 Jumbled sentences
1 How can we find out about elephants on the internet?
2 When I type in 'elephant', I get millions of results.
3 I can't read everything, and a lot of websites aren't up-to-date.
4 Yesterday I sent an e-mail to my teacher and asked her.

8 New words
1 grandma, resolution
2 card
3 I'm going to, look round, warm, weather forecast
4 Who's going to
5 Grandma
6 Grandma
7 tiger

9 The weather forecast
2 Tuesday
3 Saturday
4 Thursday
5 Friday
6 Monday
7 Wednesday

10 New words
1 download, report
2 major
3 technology, teaches
4 member
5 and so on
6 address
7 League
8 download, onto

11 Puzzle 'The internet (and so on)'
1 address
2 computer
3 website
4 screen
5 click
6 mouse
7 searched
8 send
The mystery word: *download*

12 New words
1 forgot
2 mine
3 yours
4 theirs
5 hers
6 his
7 ours

13 Whose is it?
1 mine, his
2 ours, theirs
3 yours, hers

14 New words
1 it's getting
2 got
3 switch on
4 Do you fancy, glass
5 I'm interested in
6 wrote, softball
7 high school
8 Softball
9 serious
10 Wow

15 Opposites
1 **a)** *grandma*, **b)** grandad
2 **a)** teaches, **b)** learns
3 **a)** funny, **b)** serious
4 **a)** warm, **b)** cool
5 **a)** interested, **b)** bored
6 **a)** everything, **b)** nothing

16 The weather forecast
2 clouds
3 rain
4 warmer
5 sun, hot

17 The wrong word
2 **c)** bought
3 **c)** looked round
4 **b)** taught
5 **d)** switched on
6 **b)** it's
The mystery word: *wonderful*

18 Questions and answers
1 What – c)
2 Who – d)
3 When – a)
4 How – b)
5 Where – f)
6 Why – e)

19 The fourth word
2 glass
3 yours
4 fancied
5 found
6 newspaper
7 members
8 sent

20 Making new words
z.B. *evening, every, give, he, her, here, ring, river, the, their, then, there, they, thing, three, very, …*

Unit 4

1 New words
1 blow up
2 special
3 guy
4 light, fire
5 fireworks
6 guy
7 lit, bonfire
8 burnt, fire
9 guy

2 What happened?
2 made, make
3 saw, see
4 took, take
5 lit, light
6 burnt, burn

3 New words
1 fool
2 Autumn, a bit
3 festival
4 Hindu, temples
5 candles
6 another
7 fun
8 spider
9 It's fun

4 Puzzle 'Definitions'
1 burns, candle
2 fire, burn
3 stop, festival
4 man, guy
5 come, temple
6 large, bonfire

Lösungssatz: *Autumn is the time after the summer and before Christmas.*

5 New words
1 lost
2 Cup
3 tonight
4 prize
5 a few
6 prize
7 pair of

6 The spider
2 fool
3 breakfast
4 bonfire
5 temple
6 beach

7 The right word
1 a lot of
2 no
3 a few
4 very
5 a bit
6 much

8 New words
1 plot
2 cellar
3 plotter, soldier
4 barrel, gunpowder
5 plotter, has dug, tunnel, cellar
6 barrel
7 soldier
8 God
9 cellar, empty
10 Catholic
11 gunpowder, death
12 plotter, drops, barrel
13 across
14 What's the matter

9 What do you say?
1 – b)
2 – c)
3 – f)
4 – a)
5 – d)
6 – e)

10 Odd word out
2 temple
3 tunnel
4 drive
5 plot
6 spider

11 The right word in English and German
2 into – hinein, in
3 off – weg, von … herunter
4 onto – hinauf, auf
5 across – über, hinüber
6 along – entlang

12 Missing letters
1 matter
2 cellar
3 barrel
4 soldier
5 death
6 empty
7 temple
8 candle
9 Catholic
10 spring
11 tonight
12 gunpowder

13 The right verb
1 fallen
2 gone
3 lit
4 forgotten
5 bought
6 eaten

14 New words
1 have you laid the table, yet
2 just, enough
3 I haven't washed up yet
4 already, comics
5 concert
6 I haven't lent, any

15 Puzzle
2 fun
3 prize
4 concert
5 gunpowder
6 (Lösungswort) interesting = interessant
7 fireworks
8 already
9 empty
10 dig
11 I

16 New words
1 winter
2 entrance, sweets
3 warned, tough
4 soft, sweets
5 ducks
6 Above, castle
7 castles
8 ducks
9 I was glad, sweets
10 laughed at
11 sweets, ducks
12 Ahead of
13 signal, fired, band
14 sweets
15 appetite
16 doctor

17 Picture puzzle
duck, glass, bell, castle, cup, ambulance, elephant

18 Word ladder
3 same
4 game
5 gave
6 give
7 live
8 like

19 Fire!
1 fire, gun
2 lit, fire
3 Candles, burn
4 light, bonfires
5 gunpowder, blow up

20 Word groups
2 winter
3 above
4 sweets
5 concert
6 castle

21 New words
1 We're loading, trip
2 sightseeing
3 encyclopedia

22 Crossword puzzle 'Travelling'
Across ▸ :
3 tour
4 stays
5 sightseeing
7 journey
8 guide
9 travel

Down ▾ :
1 case
2 map
3 trip
4 sights
6 tourist

23 Past participles
a) written, spoken, seen, been, rung, done

b)
(to) speak – spoke – spoken – sprechen
(to) see – saw – seen – sehen
(to) be – was/were – been – sein
(to) ring – rang – rung – anrufen
(to) do – did – done – tun

c) *Verschiedene Antworten möglich.*

24 Puzzle 'Opposites and synonyms'
2 soft
3 lend
4 man
5 glad
6 death
7 very
8 trip
9 full
10 tough
The mystery word: *forgotten*

25 Network
Verschiedene Antworten möglich.

Unit 5

1 New words
1 factory
2 jam, honey
3 deliver
4 so
5 jam
6 marmalade, jam
7 deliver

2 Definitions
a)
1 *hospital*
2 deliver
3 factory
4 dig
5 supermarket
6 build

b)
1 delivers
2 *hospital*
3 dug
4 build
5 factory
6 supermarket

3 New words
1 clothes
2 earn, office
3 market
4 sell, clean, clothes
5 earn, extra, driver
6 clothes
7 keep
8 vet
9 dirty, clothes
10 didn't get them clean

4 Verb search
2 laugh
3 get
4 sell
5 keep
6 earn
7 dig
8 deliver
9 load
10 fire
11 lay
12 copy

5 New words
1 help
2 robot
3 robot, take
4 butter, bread
5 tins, beans
6 get ready
7 purse
8 coat
9 future, will, robot
10 until, future

6 Take three
2 bag, case, purse
3 box, bottle, tin
4 factory, machine, robot
5 cake, toast, bread
6 jacket, sweater, coat

7 New words
1 arrive, soon
2 present
3 tests
4 exist
5 fair, price
6 save, without
7 potatoes
8 steal
9 That's a pity
10 damn

8 The fourth word
2 dirty
3 stolen
4 potatoes
5 animals
6 machine
7 past
8 help

9 Only two
2 take
3 cleaned
4 until
5 lent
6 clothes

10 Word web
2 soft
3 sweets
4 steal
5 spring
6 save
7 soldier
8 soon
9 sell
10 so
11 signal
12 spider

11 Pronunciation
2 [z] – [s] Ausdruck, Phrase – Rennen
3 [s] – [z] Eis – Augen
4 [s] – [z] Preis – Preis, Gewinn
5 [z] – [s] Größe – Mäuse
6 [z] – [s] Seiten – Sehenswürdigkeiten
7 [s] – [z] sitzt – Kinder

12 New words
1 trampolining
2 simple
3 ever
4 once, twice
5 etc

13 Two parts
1 – e)
2 – g)
3 – a)
4 – b)
5 – h)
6 – c)
7 – d)
8 – f)
fox, Fuchs

14 New words
1 cupboard
2 toy
3 paint
4 piece, paper
5 fixed, gate
6 broken, cassette
7 rubbish
8 sale
9 pay
10 labels
11 drink
12 lemonade

15 Partner words
cupboard – wardrobe
gate – fence
label – sign
lemonade – orange juice
meal – drink
pen – paper
piece – part
price – money
toy – game

16 The right words
2 piece, cake
3 cup, tea
4 box, cornflakes
5 glass, lemonade
6 tin, beans

17 The right verb
(2) were
(3) found
(4) sell
(5) bought
(6) saved
(7) delivered
(8) fixed
(9) painted

18 How often?
2 My sister has tried trampolining twice.
3 My mum has seen a cat in our garden three times.
4 I've played tennis once or twice.
5 We've had a caravan holiday about ten times.
6 I've done in-line skating hundreds of times.

19 Right or wrong?
2 ✘
3 ✔
4 ✘
5 ✘
6 ✔

20 Word groups
food: *bean*, bread, potato, honey, jam
jobs: driver, vet, doctor, manager, paramedic
places of work: office, bank, market, school, factory

21 Word snake
bread/drink/keep/paper/rubbish/help/potato/office/
earn/news/sponsor/robot/tough/honey/young/gate

22 Numbers and letters
1 factory
2 delivers
3 computers, robots
4 sandwiches
5 racket, garage
Lösungssatz: *Wendy has never done trampolining but she has been in a go-kart race.*

23 Missing words
1 milk
2 big
3 opens, tin
4 children, coffee
5 sit down
6 hate, marmalade
7 butter
8 better
9 trip

Unit 6

1 New words
1 teenagers, twins
2 programmes
3 soap operas
4 characters
5 comedies
6 series
7 ghost
8 cartoons
9 guests, meet, twins
10 science programme
11 tested, twins

2 Puzzle 'TV etc'
1 ghost
2 safari
3 cartoon
4 soap opera
5 comedy
6 twins
7 guests
8 series
The mystery word: *character*

3 New words
1 invited
2 become, actors, documentary
3 documentary
4 visitor, decide, round
5 became, rich
6 dinosaurs

4 Two parts
2 character
3 comedy
4 dinosaur
5 documentary
6 millionaire
7 programme
8 science
9 teenager
10 visitor

5 Missing words in jumbled sentences
2 My mother often watches the news.
3 My brother is the only family member that likes documentaries.
4 I must watch my favourite soap opera every day.
5 Only my little sister doesn't watch TV yet.

6 New words
1 dream
2 didn't understand
3 skirt
4 was expecting
5 musical instrument

7 That can't be right!
2 ~~skirt~~ shirt, ~~shirt~~ skirt
3 ~~dream~~ drama, ~~drama~~ dream
4 ~~instrument~~ advertisement, ~~advertisement~~ instrument

8 "ex"-words
2 exciting
3 explain
4 expensive
5 expect
6 extra

9 New words
1 when, middle
2 inside, turned
3 had to, get to, main
4 followed
5 almost
6 maze, hedges
7 get lost
8 turning
9 dead end
10 probably, missed
11 between

10 Odd word out
1 middle
2 main
3 dream
4 ghost
5 millionaire
6 maze

11 Where's the ball?
1 between
2 behind
3 on
4 under
5 in front of
6 inside

12 The right word
1 **a)** lost, **b)** clean
2 **a)** almost, **b)** always
3 **a)** between, **b)** before
4 **a)** turn, **b)** earn
5 **a)** really, **b)** probably
6 **a)** missed, **b)** lost
7 **a)** as, **b)** if

13 New words
1 ears
2 mouth, nose
3 describe
4 tall
5 eyes
6 jeans
7 face

14 Funny Face

a)

1 nose, nose
2 eyes
3 ear
4 mouth, mouth
5 head, head
6 hair

b) *Verschiedene Antworten möglich.*

15 New words

1 nervous
2 record
3 channel
4 traffic
5 favour, well
6 should, tape
7 rest
8 recorded, tape, worth
9 fault
10 mean
11 dialled

16 Situations

1 That's a pity.
2 Yes, but it wasn't my fault.
3 Well, I think you should buy the yellow T-shirt.
4 That's easy. Look. You just have to read the answers first.

17 Missing letters

2 tape – soap
3 fault – should
4 record – worth
5 traffic – office
6 caravan – paragraph
7 become – between
8 favour – nervous
9 tunnel – channel
10 candle – middle

18 Find the mistakes

1 *yesterday* ▸ *today*, policeman ▸ policewoman
2 Their ▸ There, letter ▸ number
3 have ▸ has, threw ▸ through
4 record ▸ remember, drives ▸ drive
5 driver ▸ drivers, favour ▸ fault
6 no ▸ some, becourse ▸ because

19 Adjective puzzle

mean, nervous, tall, rich, broken, simple, fair, clean

20 Odd word out

2 say
3 year
4 lose
5 where
6 maze

21 Silly sentence

She should probably do me a favour and invite a guest inside our maze.

22 Word families

a)

2 sell, sale
3 test, test
4 turn, turning
5 act, actor
6 drive, driver
7 teach, teacher
8 visit, visitor

b)

2 turning
3 actor
4 sell
5 visitors
6 test

23 Word friends

1 *go home*, go to school
2 have a party, have fun
3 keep back, keep cows
4 look after, look round

24 Network

Verschiedene Antworten möglich.

25 Missing words

1 trip
2 tough
3 as, entrance
4 inside
5 find, middle
6 lost
7 bit
8 glad
9 easy
10 well
11 faster
12 hedges

Unit 7

1 New words

1 state
2 state
3 Huge, golden, deserts
4 movies
5 resort
6 waterfalls, ridges, national
7 ski

2 What do you mean?
1 resort
2 ridge
3 desert
4 surfing

3 New words
1 steep, hill, cable car, below
2 Gulf Stream
3 island, ocean
4 ocean
5 endless, highways, land
6 wine, Valley

4 Groups of words
1 *country, land,* state
2 highway, road, street
3 hill, mountain, ridge
4 lake, ocean, sea

5 New words
1 lots of, spelling
2 gas, petrol, truck, lorry
3 french fries
4 mail
5 vacation

6 British and American English
a)
main road → *highway*, neighbours → neighbors, chips → french fries, programmes → programs, petrol station → gas station

b)
vacation, trucks, center, movies, color

7 New words
1 players
2 welcome
3 Meanwhile
4 sounds, Mom
5 position
6 catcher
7 equipment

8 English words in Germany
Clothes: cap, jeans, …
Food, etc: barbecue, burger, …
Spare time: camping, comic, party, …
Sports: bowling, basketball, surfing, …
Technology, etc: computer, download, internet, smartphone, website, …
Other words: jet lag, teenager, ticket, …

Verschiedene ergänzende Antworten möglich.

9 New words
1 batter
2 pitcher
3 hit
4 pitcher
5 pitcher, batter
6 garbage
7 recycle

10 Puzzle 'People who do things'
1 singer
2 pitcher
3 player
4 driver
5 batter
6 teacher
7 catcher
8 footballer
9 manager
The mystery word: *stretcher*

11 New words
1 kiss
2 friendly
3 explanation
4 square
5 building
6 Exactly
7 splash
8 Good luck

12 Word families
a)
2 explanation
3 camp
4 sound
5 end
6 friendly
7 fun
8 lucky

b)
1 sounded
2 funny
3 explanation
4 friendly
5 building

13 Puzzle
1 hit
2 exact
3 garbage
4 equipment
5 explanation
6 meanwhile
7 mission
8 steep
9 ski
The mystery word: *interesting*

14 The fourth word

2 swim
3 gas
4 catch
5 below
6 cap
7 correct
8 post

15 "re"-words

2 resolution
3 remember
4 result
5 repeat
6 report
7 recycle

16 Three words

1 *island* / resort / valley
2 burgers / french fries / potatoes
3 bowling / camping / surfing
4 batter / catcher / pitcher
5 friendly / mean / nervous
6 hit / splash / stop

17 Missing words

1 holiday
2 small
3 nothing, boring
4 shops
5 films, cinemas
6 lie, day
7 fantastic/great, friendly, man
8 gives
9 lend
10 post

Extra

1 A "crossverb" puzzle

Across ▸ :

1 understand
5 earn
6 miss
8 painting
10 following
11 turns
13 paid
14 existed
17 arrive
19 become
21 sold
23 saving
24 keeps

Down ▾ :

2 describe
3 delivers
4 dialled
7 invited
9 sounds
12 stolen
14 expects
15 decide
16 fixed
18 met
20 took
22 hit

2 Secret messages

1 Would you like to go to the cinema with me tomorrow?
2 Somebody is waiting for you at the main entrance of the school.
3 Can we go to the birthday party together?
4 Come and meet me at the garden gate tonight.